How to Use

MICROSOFT
WINDOWS NT 4
WORKSTATION

How to Use

MICROSOFT WINDOWS NT 4 WORKSTATION

JACQUELYN GAVRON AND JOSEPH MORAN

Ziff Davis Press
An imprint of Macmillan Computer Publishing USA
Emeryville, California

Acquisitions Editor	Lysa Lewallen
Copy Editor	Kim Haglund
Technical Reviewer	Ron Pacchiano
Book Design	Dennis Gallagher/Visual Strategies, San Francisco
Technical Illustration	Dave Feasey, Sarah Ishida, and Mina Reimer
Word Processing	Howard Blechman
Page Layout	Martha Barrera
Indexer	Christine Spina

Ziff-Davis Press imprint books are produced on a Macintosh computer system with the following applications: FrameMaker®, Microsoft® Word, QuarkXPress®, Adobe Illustrator®, Adobe Photoshop®, Adobe Streamline™, MacLink® *Plus*, Aldus® FreeHand™, Collage Plus™.

Screen shots reprinted by permission from Microsoft Corporation.

Ziff-Davis Press, an imprint of
Macmillan Computer Publishing USA
5903 Christie Avenue
Emeryville, CA 94608

This book was produced digitally by Macmillan Computer Publishing and manufactured using 100% computer-to-plate technology (filmless process), by Shepard Poorman Communications Corporation, Indianapolis, Indiana.

ISBN 1-56276-445-4

Manufactured in the United States of America
10 9 8 7 6 5 4 3 2

To Danielle Samolewicz
and Joseph Polauf,
for their patience
and understanding

TABLE OF CONTENTS

Contents of '3½ Floppy (A:)'

ACKNOWLEDGMENTS

 We'd like to thank several people for their help and support while we were writing this book: Jim Louderback, Lysa Lewallen, Juliet Langley, Sue Ng, Ron Pacchiano, and especially David Chernicoff.

INTRODUCTION

How to Use Microsoft Windows NT 4 Workstation is an illustrated, step-by-step guide to using the newest version of the Windows operating system. Whether you're using Windows for the first time or upgrading to Windows NT 4 from an earlier version of the operating system—Windows 3.1, Windows NT 3.51, or Windows 95—you'll find everything you need to get up to speed with the new operating system as quickly as possible. *How to Use Microsoft Windows NT 4 Workstation* takes a hands-on approach, walking you through each step involved in tasks such as updating documents with My Briefcase, installing and removing applications, and setting up your desktop to look and run the way you like it. Each step is accompanied by screen shots that mirror what you'll see on your computer's monitor.

If you're upgrading to Windows NT 4 from Windows 3.1 or NT 3.51, the first thing you'll notice about Windows NT 4 is that it's got a completely different user interface. To introduce you to all these new icons and tools, we begin with the basics: getting started, finding your way around Windows NT, managing files and folders, and working with applications (including those that come with Windows NT). Of course, the look and feel isn't all that's new in Windows NT 4. It's got most everything you need to get on line as well, including a browser called the Internet Explorer. Here you'll find a comprehensive guide to using Windows NT to access the World Wide Web, from setting up your modem to customizing IE and surfing to actual Web sites. Later chapters cover topics ranging from protecting your data and customizing the desktop to networking (which is just one of Windows NT's many strengths). In addition, all chapters contain Tip Sheets with hints and tricks that offer alternative ways to perform various tasks and reveal features and functions that are highly useful but not evident from mere mousing around. Bottom line? By the time you finish *How to Use Microsoft Windows NT 4 Workstation,* you'll know the ins and outs of Windows NT 4 and be able to work with it quickly and efficiently.

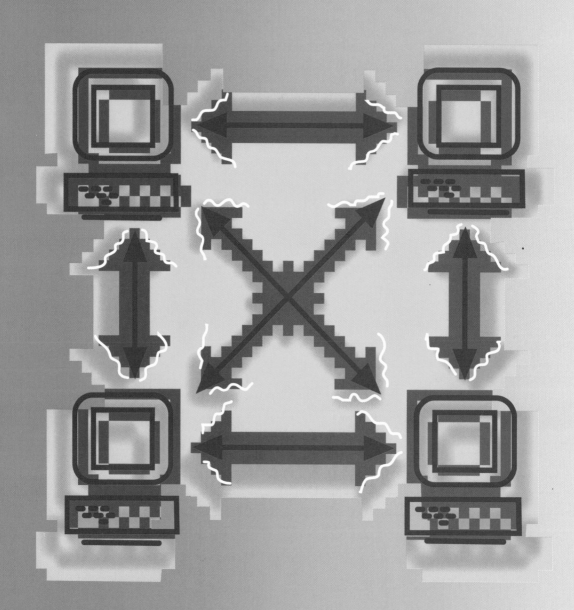

CHAPTER 1

Getting Started with Windows NT

 Every time you use Windows NT 4, there are a few basic tasks you'll *always* have to do: log on and log off the system, and shut down (turn off) your computer. In this chapter, you'll learn how to perform these basic tasks. You'll also learn why Windows NT is such a secure environment and how to take advantage of its security. Windows NT was designed, from the ground up, with security in mind. For this reason, it lets you create a separate logon account for each colleague (or family member) sharing your computer. The benefit is that Windows NT 4 automatically saves all the preferences (such as screen savers or desktop layout) associated with each logon account. So if you like the 3D Flying Objects screen saver and your partner likes 3D Flowerbox, you can each have it your own way.

More importantly, Windows NT 4 lets you put certain files off limits to other users. So if you don't want someone to read that confidential memo you wrote, you can restrict access to that file.

How to Log on to Windows NT 4

To get started using Windows NT 4, the first thing you must do is log on to your computer by entering a username and a password. In doing so, you identify yourself to Windows NT 4, which makes sure that all your unique preferences, such as the type of wallpaper or the layout of the desktop, are activated when Windows NT starts. Windows NT also uses the username and password to control access to various items on the system, including applications and files.

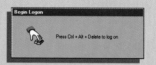

1 Turn on your computer. When Windows NT 4 finishes loading, it displays a logon dialog box that tells you to press Ctrl+Alt+Delete, which you should do.

4 If everything goes smoothly, you will now be ready to use Windows NT 4. This screen—commonly called the *desktop*—contains several icons: My Computer, Network Neighborhood, My Briefcase, Internet Explorer, Inbox, and Recycle Bin. (See Chapter 2 to learn how to use each of these icons.)

TIP SHEET

▶ **If you forget your password, you can't access Windows NT 4. (It's not like Windows 95, which lets you bypass the logon screen by pressing the Escape key.) If you're attached to a network, you'll have to call the network administrator, who'll create a new password for you (not even the administrator knows your password!). If you're not attached to a network, you have no choice but to reinstall Windows NT 4. To learn how to change your password, see Chapter 14.**

2 Now the Logon Information dialog box appears. In it, you must type both your username and your password. When you're done, click OK. (See the Tip Sheet if you forget your password.)

3 If your username and password are valid, the Windows NT 4 desktop will appear in a few seconds. If not, you'll be presented with an error message that reads "The system could not log you on. Make sure your User name and domain are correct, then type in your password again. Letters in passwords must be typed using the correct case. Make sure that Caps Lock is not accidentally on."

How to Log off Windows NT 4

If you're not going to be using your machine for an extended period of time (when you leave work for the day, for example), you should always log off Windows NT 4. Logging off closes open applications and prepares Windows NT for another user. It's also a security measure that prevents unauthorized users from using your Windows NT account—and all the applications and files you have access to.

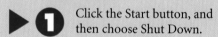

▶ **1** Click the Start button, and then choose Shut Down.

TIP SHEET

▶ **If you're going to be away from your system for only a short period of time and you don't want to log off, you can** *lock* **your workstation. Like logging off, locking your workstation prevents unauthorized users from using your account— but your applications remain open so you can get back to work quickly. To lock your workstation, press Ctrl+Alt+Delete, then click the Lock Workstation button. To regain access to Windows NT, you'll have to reenter your password (but not your username).**

▶ **Although Windows NT is a very stable operating system, there may be times when the system fails to respond and won't accept input from the mouse. If this occurs, press Ctrl+Alt+Delete. Doing so displays a dialog box called Windows NT Security, which has a button that reads "Shut Down." Click it to shut down.**

2 The Shut Down Windows dialog box appears. It presents you with the three options you see in this screen.

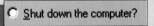

3 You can turn off the PC for the night by choosing "Shut down the computer." It takes Windows NT 4 a few seconds to do this; when it's finished, a dialog box tells you it's safe to turn off your computer. This dialog box also has a Restart button, which you'll need to click when you're ready to use Windows NT 4 again.

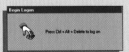

4 The second option is to restart the computer, which you should use only if your system is behaving erratically and you want to see if restarting will fix the problem.

5 Use the third option, "Close all programs and log on as a different user," if you're sharing the computer with other users. When you choose this option, Windows NT 4 automatically closes your account. The next user then must press Ctrl+Alt+Delete, which opens the Logon Information screen where they'll enter their username and password.

How to Get Help in Windows NT

Windows NT comes with an online help system that can answer questions about the operating system and help you solve just about any problem you experience.

 1 To open the help system, click the Start button, then choose Help from the Start menu.

8 To print the contents of an online help file, click the Options button in the Windows NT Help window and then select Print Topic.

7 Press the Display button. Once Windows NT has found the topic you need help with, you'll see a window like this one.

TIP SHEET

▶ By default, help windows stay on top of all other windows. If you don't want help windows to behave this way, click the Options button in the help window you're using. Select Keep Help on Top, then choose the item that reads Not on Top.

▶ To change the size of the help window fonts, click the Options button in the help window you're using. Then select the Font option, which gives you three choices: Small, Normal, and Large. (Normal is the one NT uses by default.)

2 When the help system opens, you'll see three tabs: Contents, Index, and Find. Each lets you search for information a different way.

3 To search for information by topic, click on the Index tab, which displays an index like the one at the back of a book. In the blank space at the top of the dialog box, type in either the entire word or just the first few letters of the word you're interested in. As soon as you start typing, the Index list jumps to that topic.

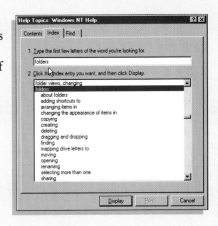

4 To search for information by category, click on the Contents tab. Here, you double-click the topic you need help with rather than typing in a word, as you would using the Index tab.

6 Windows NT is now ready to create the database, or list, of terms. Click the Finish button to generate the list. When it's done, the Find tab appears. Now just type the word (or words) that best describes what you need help with—in this example it's *folders*.

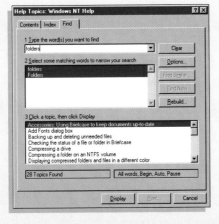

5 If you can't find the information you need using the Index and Contents tabs, click the Find tab. This displays the Find Setup Wizard, which generates a list of *all* words in the entire help system. You can then search this list using words or phrases. Minimize creates a small list. Maximize creates a larger database, one that's more likely to contain the terms you need. Choose the option you want, then click Next.

CHAPTER 2

Using the Windows NT 4 Desktop

Whether you're using Windows NT 4 for the first time, or upgrading to it from DOS, Windows 3.1, Windows for Workgroups 3.11, or Windows NT 3.51, the changes are evident from the moment you log on. Instead of Windows 3.1's Program Manager and File Manager folders, several icons appear down the left side of the screen: My Computer, Network Neighborhood, and Recycle Bin. Along the bottom of the screen is a horizontal bar—called the *Taskbar*—and on it is the all-important Start button. As the name implies, the Start button is key, because it's used to access all the programs you install on your computer as well as those that come with Windows NT 4. The Taskbar lets you know, at a glance, which applications you have open; you'll also use it to switch among open applications. By the time you finish this chapter, you'll have mastered not only the Start button and Taskbar, but the Recycle Bin and My Computer. If your computer is attached to a local area network, or *LAN*, you'll know how to use Network Neighborhood, too.

There are other icons on the desktop as well: Inbox (for sending and receiving e-mail); Internet Explorer (for surfing the World Wide Web); and My Briefcase (for updating files you work with at home or on the road). For more information on these icons, see Chapters 8 ("Using a Modem") and 12 ("Using NT with Notebook Computers.")

One final note before you begin: here and in the chapters that follow you'll be asked to "right-click" an icon (or the desktop). That simply means you should place the cursor over the icon and press the right mouse button.

How to Use the Start Button

The Start button is like a dashboard: It contains all the controls you need to operate Windows NT 4. For example, you can launch the programs installed on your computer (including DOS programs) and access all of Windows NT 4's built-in applications, such as the Calculator, Control Panel applets, and NT Explorer. If you're upgrading to Windows NT 4 from Windows 3.1, Windows for Workgroups 3.11, or NT 3.51, all of your program groups will appear as folders on the Start button's Programs menu.

Start button **Start menu**

1 To open the Start menu, click the Start button. The small black arrow to the right of Programs, Documents, Settings, and Find indicates that there's another menu beneath each item; to view any of these menus, simply glide the mouse over the item. For example, selecting Programs opens a secondary menu containing all the programs installed on your system.

Start button

7 Like almost every other object on your Windows NT 4 desktop, the Start button opens a context menu when you right-click it. The first option, Open, reveals a window containing folders for all the programs you can access from the Start button. Explore launches the NT Explorer, and Find launches Window NT 4's utility for locating files and folders.

TIP SHEET

▶ **Another way to open the Start menu is by pressing the Ctrl+Esc keys.**

▶ **Many newer keyboards have a key with the Windows logo on it to the left of the spacebar. Pressing this key also opens the Start menu.**

▶ **To remove the contents of the Documents menu, click on the Start button, then choose Settings and then Taskbar. In the Taskbar Properties window that pops open, choose Start Menu Programs. Then click on the Clear button, and choose OK. The Documents menu should now be empty.**

▶ **A fast way to add a program to the top of the Start menu is to drag the program's icon to the Start button from within the NT Explorer. (To access the NT Explorer, click the Start button, then Programs.)**

2 Place the mouse over Accessories, and you'll see yet another menu with all Windows NT 4's built-in programs, such as Calculator, WordPad, and HyperTerminal.

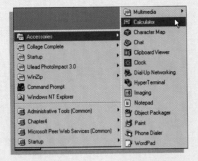

3 To run DOS programs, open the Start menu, select Programs, and then Command Prompt. A window for launching DOS programs opens. To close it, type Exit at the c: prompt.

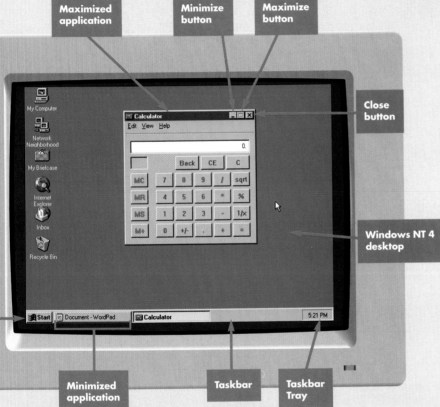

Maximized application

Minimize button

Maximize button

Close button

Windows NT 4 desktop

Minimized application

Taskbar

Taskbar Tray

4 To access Windows NT 4's online documentation, select Help from the Start menu. The help system gives you several ways to search for assistance. On the Index tab, for example, you can type in the word that best describes the topic you're interested in. Or, click the Contents tab and search for help by Category.

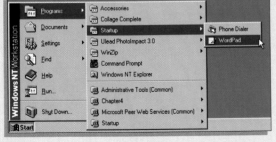

5 To quickly open a document you've worked on recently, select Documents from the Start button. You'll then see a menu listing the files you last worked with. Click on the one you want to open.

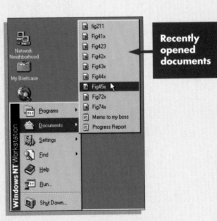

Recently opened documents

6 Under Programs is a folder called Startup. Applications placed in the Startup folder launch automatically when you start Windows NT 4. It's useful to add to the Startup folder those programs you use daily—a word processor or the Internet Explorer, for instance. To learn how to add programs to Startup, see Chapter 11, "Customizing Windows NT 4."

How to Use the Taskbar

In Windows 3.11 and NT 3.51, there was no easy way to identify which applications were open. If one application was maximized, or if windows overlapped, you had to press the Alt+Tab keys or tediously minimize each open application to determine how many applications were running. Fortunately, Windows NT 4 cleans up the mess with the Taskbar, a horizontal bar along the bottom of the desktop that uses buttons to represent all open applications.

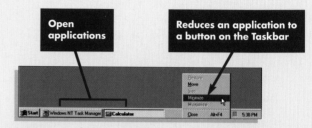

▶ **1** A quick glance at the Taskbar shows which applications are running. To switch among them, just click any button and that application moves to the foreground. To hide an application window, right-click its button on the Taskbar and select Minimize.

TIP SHEET

▶ **If you have a lot of applications open at once, Windows NT reduces the size of their buttons to make them all fit on the Taskbar. But in doing so, it truncates the text label, making it difficult to identify the application the button represents. To see the entire label, place the cursor over a Taskbar button and, a second or so later, a small label with the entire name visible pops open.**

▶ **Old habits die hard: You can still use Alt+Tab to switch from one application to another.**

▶ **Some applications, such anti-virus programs and the Windows NT Task Manager, install themselves on the Taskbar's Tray. This allows fast, easy access so you can continually monitor the information they track. The Task Manager, for example, can monitor the performance of your system, displaying information such as the amount of memory that's currently in use.**

▶ **To move the Taskbar to any side of the screen place the cursor on the Taskbar. While pressing the left mouse button drag it to its new location.**

2 You can also use the Taskbar to neatly arrange windows on the screen. Right-click any blank space on the Taskbar and use the menu that appears to arrange windows in one of three ways: overlapping one another (Cascade Windows), stacked (Tile Windows Horizontally), or side-by-side (Tile Windows Vertically).

Cascade Windows
Tile Windows Horizontally
Tile Windows Vertically

Minimize All Windows

Task Manager...

Properties

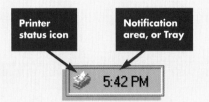

Printer status icon

Notification area, or Tray

5:42 PM

3 To the extreme right of the Taskbar is a notification area called the Tray. It displays information including the time of day and the status of certain peripheral devices such as a modem and a printer.

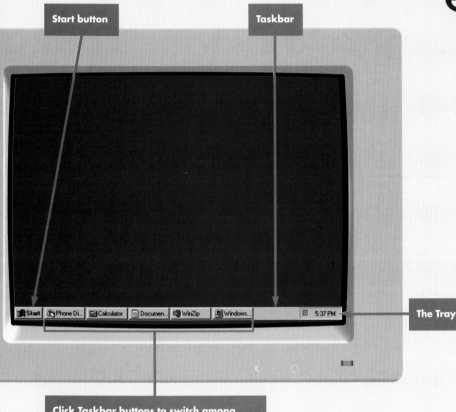

Start button

Taskbar

The Tray

Click Taskbar buttons to switch among open applications, folders, and documents.

4 To control the way the Taskbar behaves, right-click a blank section and select Properties from the menu that opens. From the Taskbar Options tab, you can specify whether the Taskbar is to remain visible at all times (Always on top). For a less cluttered desktop, you can set the Taskbar so that it appears only when you move the cursor to the bottom of your screen (Auto hide). You can also remove the clock by deselecting the Show Clock option so that the check mark beside it disappears.

5 To clean up the desktop really fast, right-click any blank section of the Taskbar and select Minimize All Windows. Next thing you know, the desktop will be empty, though all applications are still running and accessible from the Taskbar.

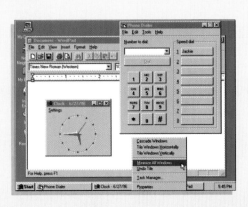

How to Use My Computer

My Computer contains icons to represent almost all the storage devices attached to your computer: the hard disk, floppy, CD-ROM, and network drives. By double-clicking these icons, you can examine their contents. In My Computer you'll also find Printers and Control Panel folders, as well as a Dial-Up Networking icon, for connecting to remote networks via modem.

► **1** Double-click My Computer to view all the storage devices attached to your PC, as shown in the central graphic on this page.

TIP SHEET

▸ As you explore drives from the My Computer icon, the screen fills with folder windows. By default, each new folder opens another window. However, you can set My Computer to use one window instead of a new one each time. Right click My Computer, choose Properties, and click the Folder tab. Select the option that reads "Browse folders by using a single window that changes as you open each folder."

▸ If you press the Backspace key while a folder window is open, you jump back to the parent folder. Keep pressing it, and you can navigate back up to My Computer.

2 Right-click the My Computer icon and select Properties. Doing so opens a dialog box that tells you the version of NT that's running, the person to whom it's registered, the type of processor in your PC, and the amount of memory that's installed in it.

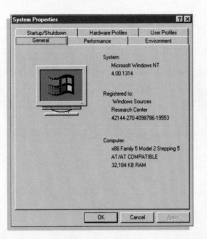

3 To examine the contents of a particular drive, double-click its icon. You'll then see a window filled with folders. To drill down, double-click a folder and you'll see the files it contains.

Floppy drive

Hard-disk drive

CD-ROM drive

Network drive

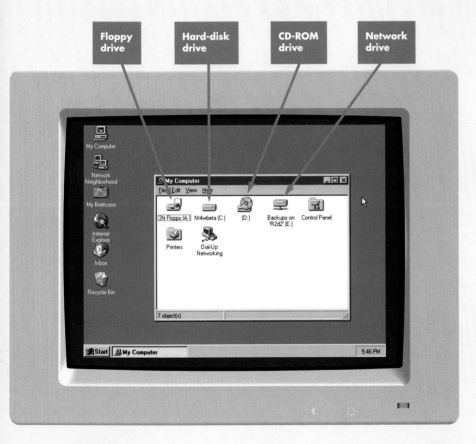

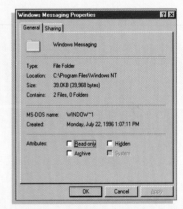

4 To uncover information about a particular folder, such as its size or how many files it contains, right-click it and then choose Properties.

6 Now type in a new name and press Enter.

5 To really make it *your* computer, rename the My Computer icon. Just right-click it and then choose Rename from the menu that appears.

How to Use Recycle Bin

In Windows 3.11 and Windows NT 3.51, there was no easy way to recover files you deleted. To do so, you had to use a third-party utility such as Symantec's Norton Desktop. Windows NT 4, however, has a Recycle Bin. When you delete files or folders, they aren't immediately erased, but sent to the Recycle Bin, which stores them for a predefined period of time. So if you accidentally delete a file, you can recover it simply by opening the Recycle Bin and dragging it out onto the desktop.

▶ **1** Double-click the Recycle Bin icon to view a list of all the documents you've deleted.

2 Right-click any file in the Recycle Bin and a context menu pops open. From here, you can return a file to its original location (Restore); copy it to the Clipboard (Cut); or re-move it from Recycle Bin entirely (Delete).

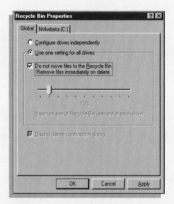

3 Right-click the Recycle Bin icon and choose Properties. The Global tab lets you determine how much hard-disk space the Recycle Bin will consume. (Remember, if you don't delete files from the Recycle Bin, they're wasting space.) To by-pass the Recycle Bin and delete documents immediately, choose the option you see checked in the screen above.

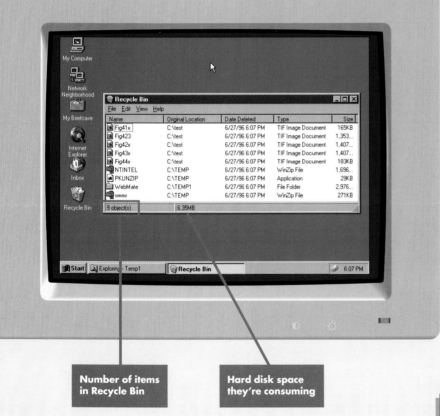

Number of items in Recycle Bin

Hard disk space they're consuming

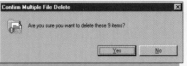

4 Whenever you empty the Recycle Bin, a win-dow pops open and confirms whether you re-ally want to delete the files. Though this is a useful safety measure, it gets annoying fast. To avoid seeing this dialog box, uncheck the op-tion in the Recycle Bin Properties window that reads "Display delete confirmation dialog."

How to Use Network Neighborhood

If your computer is connected to a network, the Network Neighborhood icon will appear on your desktop. While My Computer displays all the drives located in your PC, Network Neighborhood lets you browse and access other computers attached to the network. This is helpful if files and folders you need are stored on a networked computer rather than locally on your hard disk. When you double-click Network Neighborhood, a window opens displaying icons representing all computers in your *workgroup*—that is, the part of the network that your machine is connected to. (Large corporate networks can get pretty complex and are often made up of many workgroups.)

 1 Double-click Network Neighborhood and you'll see a window containing icons for all other computers in your *workgroup*. It may take a second or so for these icons to display.

TIP SHEET

▶ If you don't see the Network Neighborhood icon on the desktop, it means you're not connected to a network.

▶ To learn how to connect to another computer on the network, see Chapter 13, "Networking."

▶ To create a shortcut to any machine in the Network Neighborhood window, right-click and drag that machine to the desktop. Then select Create Shortcut(s) Here from the menu that appears. The shortcut lets you access the machine without having to open the Network Neighborhood, saving a few mouse clicks in the process.

2 The Network Neighborhood window also contains an icon called Entire Network, which displays all other machines on the network, but which are not part of your workgroup.

3 To see the contents of a networked computer, double-click its icon. If you haven't logged on to the machine, Windows NT 4 will ask you to do so.

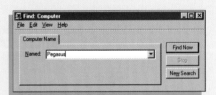

4 If you know that the files you need are on a particular computer, you can avoid browsing and find that computer quickly using Windows NT 4's Find tool. To do this, right-click Network Neighborhood and choose Find Computer from the menu. You'll need to know the name of the computer you're looking for; type this name in the blank area (here, the computer's name is Pegasus) and press Enter (or click Find Now) to start the search.

5 To learn the name of your computer and workgroup—also called a *domain*—right-click Network Neighborhood and select Properties from the menu. The Identification window contains this information.

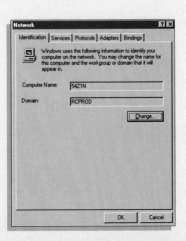

CHAPTER 3

Working with Applications

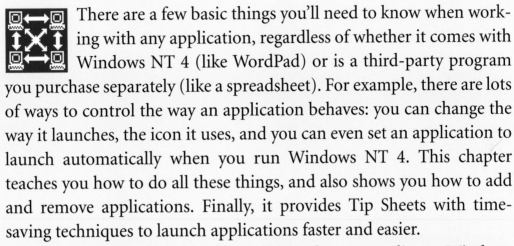 There are a few basic things you'll need to know when working with any application, regardless of whether it comes with Windows NT 4 (like WordPad) or is a third-party program you purchase separately (like a spreadsheet). For example, there are lots of ways to control the way an application behaves: you can change the way it launches, the icon it uses, and you can even set an application to launch automatically when you run Windows NT 4. This chapter teaches you how to do all these things, and also shows you how to add and remove applications. Finally, it provides Tip Sheets with time-saving techniques to launch applications faster and easier.

Before you continue, one note to those of you upgrading to Windows NT 4 from earlier versions of Windows. Windows NT 4 uses slightly different buttons to control application windows. In the upper-right corner of every application are, from left to right, buttons to minimize, maximum, and close applications. These buttons are present in virtually every dialog box and window you see in Windows NT 4.

How to Add and Remove Applications

In Windows 3.11, there was no automatic way to install applications: You had to manually locate an application's setup (or install) routine and launch it yourself. Fortunately, Windows NT 4 automates the task with an Add/Remove Programs applet in the Control Panel. There's no magic involved: It just searches for a SETUP.EXE or INSTALL.EXE file on the root directory of the floppy and CD-ROM drives. You can use this applet to install or remove components of an application or of Windows NT itself. For example, if you chose Typical when you installed Windows NT 4, not all operating system components were loaded onto your hard disk, including the animated mouse pointers. Here, you'll learn how to install them; the same steps apply to installing any program.

TIP SHEET

▶ **With earlier versions of Windows, to remove an application you either had to know all the files it installed or else use a third-party uninstall utility. Windows NT 4, however, has a built-in uninstall utility that can automatically remove some applications. Which ones? Well, if the application's name appears in the Install/Uninstall tab's window (see step 5, which displays Ulead PhotoImpact), then Windows NT 4 can indeed remove it automatically. To start the uninstall process, click the application you want to remove, then click the Add/Remove button. Windows NT then removes all the files the application installed initially.**

▶ **1** Click on Start, Settings, and then Control Panel. Doing so opens the Control Panel window. Now launch the Add/Remove Programs icon by double-clicking it.

7 Windows NT locates the installation file, which in this example is IN-STALL.EXE. (If Windows Windows NT can't find the file, you'll have to click Browse  and find it as you did using Windows 3.11.) Now click Finish, and you're done.

6 You'll see the first in a series of screens that walks you through the install process: It asks you to insert the floppy or CD-ROM disk. Do so, then click the Next button.

2 You'll now see a dialog box with two tabs: Install/Uninstall and Windows NT Setup. Because you'll be installing a component of Windows NT, click the Windows Windows NT Setup tab. (The Install/Uninstall tab is for adding and removing separate, third-party applications—a word processor or spreadsheet, for example. You'll learn how to do this a bit later.).

Minimize button

Maximize button

Close button

3 Double-click Accessories to open a list of all the extra software Windows NT 4 comes with (clicking the Details button also opens this list). Click on the box beside Mouse Pointers; a check mark appears. To the right of this item Windows NT 4 indicates the amount of disk space this component requires; below the Components list it indicates the amount of space available on your hard disk. Click OK to return to the Windows NT Setup tab. Click OK again to begin installing Mouse Pointers.

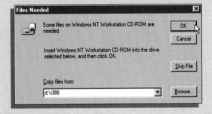

4 Windows NT 4 prompts you to insert the Windows NT 4 CD. In the blank area type the directory where the files it needs are located: d:\i386. (i386 is the directory where Windows NT stores all its files, so you'll access it no matter what component you're installing.) Windows NT then copies the files it needs and reports on its progress. You're done!

5 If you're installing a program such as a word processor or spreadsheet, the process is a bit different. First, you'll be using the Install/Uninstall tab. Switch to that tab, then click the Install button.

How to Launch Applications

When you install applications under Windows NT 4, their icons will appear in the Program's menu that opens when you click the Start button. Selecting a program from this menu is the easiest way to start one up. However, there are several other ways to get the job done: You can create shortcuts on the desktop (which saves a few mouse clicks), double-click an application's icon from within the Windows NT Explorer, or launch it from the command line. Here, you'll learn how to launch applications three ways, and later in this chapter, you'll learn how to launch them using shortcuts. When you finish this chapter, you'll have a whole slew of techniques for starting applications. The choice is yours.

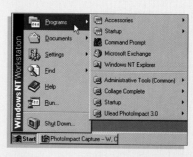

▶ **1** The easiest way to launch an application is from the Start menu. Click the Start button, then choose Programs. The menu that opens contains both individual applications (like Windows NT Explorer) and program groups (like Accessories). To launch Windows NT Explorer, just click on it.

2 If, however, you want to launch a program that resides within a program group, glide the mouse over the item. All programs within that group then appear. Sometimes, there are even groups within groups. Accessories, for instance, contains several other program groups: Hyperterminal, Multimedia, and System Tools. (You can always tell when there are subgroups because a black arrow appears beside the item.)

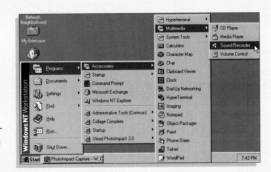

3 As you learned in step 2, Windows NT 4 often nests programs deep within the Start menu. If you use an application often, all those mouse clicks get tiresome. That's where shortcuts come in. To learn how to create a shortcut to launch an application, see "How to Create Shortcuts to Applications" later in this chapter.

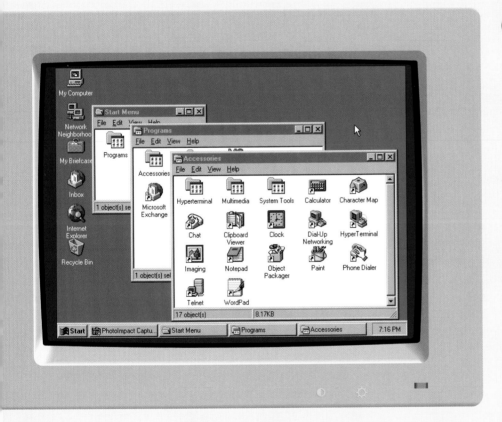

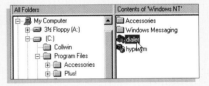

4 Another way to launch applications is by using the Windows NT Explorer. Open it, find the program you want to launch, and then double-click it.

5 Finally, you can also launch applications using the Start menu's Run command. Just click the Start button, choose Run, and either type in the name of the program, or click the Browse button to locate it.

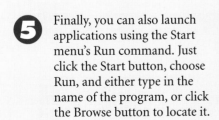

How to Control an Application's Launch Window

O nce you've launched an application, you can use the Taskbar to minimize or maximize its window. However, you can also set an application to launch in either minimized or maximized mode. This is useful if, for example, you always want your word processor to launch maximized, so you can view as much text as possible. On the other hand, you might want a program you use less frequently, perhaps an e-mail package, to launch minimized, so that it's running but doesn't take up valuable space on your desktop.

TIP SHEET

▶ **To launch an application with a single keystroke, first open the Shortcut tab, then click within the field labeled Shortcut Key. Now press the key, or keys, you want to use to launch the application. You can use almost any key, or any combination of keys, that you wish. Click OK, and you're done. One reminder: Some keystroke combinations are off limits. For example, Windows NT 4 reserves some keystroke combinations for its own use, such as Ctrl+Alt+Delete.**

▶ **To change an application's icon, click the Change Icon button at the bottom of the Shortcut tab (see step 5). Windows NT 4 then displays a Change Icon window that highlights the icon currently representing the application. If there are other icons to choose from, they'll appear in the Current Icon window. (If not, you can either browse for icons or else stick with the one you've got.) Select the new icon, and click OK to close the Shortcut tab. Then click OK again to close the Properties window. The new icon will now replace the old one.**

▶ **1** To specify whether an application launches in a maximized or a minimized window, click on the Start button, then choose Settings and Taskbar.

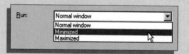

6 The bottom half of the Shortcut tab contains a section labeled Run. Click on the arrow to the right of the field; this opens a pick list with three options: Normal window (the default), Minimized, and Maximized. Choose the option you want, click OK, and you're done. From now on, the application will launch the way you specified.

2 The Taskbar Properties dialog box opens. Click the Start Menu Programs tab.

3 Click the Advanced button. This launches the Windows NT Explorer and automatically lands you in the Programs folder in the right pane.

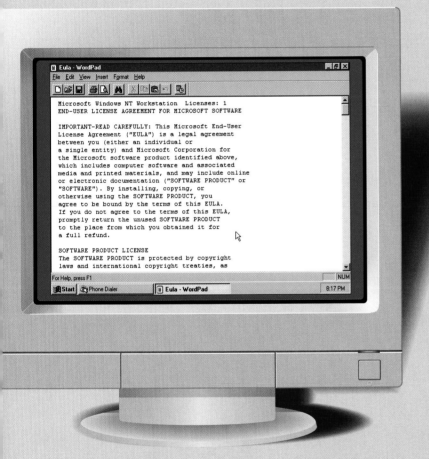

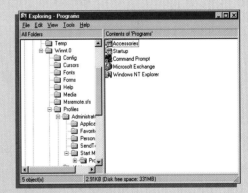

4 Double-click the Programs folder. You'll now see folders representing each individual application and each group of applications.

5 Now, you're ready to change the way an application launches. First, right-click the application, and then select Properties from the menu that appears. Next, click on the Shortcut tab. (This example displays the Properties window for Windows NT Explorer.)

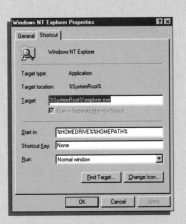

How to Create Shortcuts to Applications

S hortcuts are one of the most useful features in Windows NT 4 because they can really save time (and mouse clicks). A shortcut allows you to quickly launch applications directly from the desktop, rather than wading through the Start menu or the Windows NT Explorer. In fact, you can create a shortcut to just about any object, including applications, printers, disk drives, and folders. There are several ways to create shortcuts. Here, you'll learn the easiest and most reliable methods.

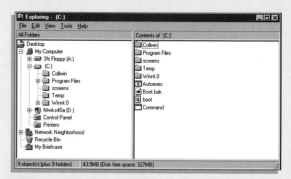

▶ **1** To create a shortcut to a document or an application, first open Windows NT Explorer.

TIP SHEET

▶ **To locate the file or document to which you want to create a shortcut, use the Find utility on the Start menu. Or, pull down the Windows NT Explorer's Tools menu, then choose Find.**

▶ **Another way to create a shortcut to any object is to use the right mouse button to drag it to the desktop (or to another folder). Then choose Create Shortcut(s) from the menu that pops open.**

▶ **Another way to delete a shortcut is to drag it to the Recycle Bin.**

▶ **To create a shortcut in a folder, open Windows NT Explorer's File menu. Choose New, then Shortcut. You're then prompted to type the location of the item you want a shortcut to, and a name for the shortcut.**

2 Locate the application or document you need (see the Tip Sheet below). When you've found it, right click its icon and select Create Shortcut from the menu that appears.

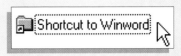

3 A shortcut to the object will now appear in the Explorer's right pane.

4 Now drag the shortcut from the Windows NT explorer onto the Desktop.

Shortcut arrow

Printer shortcut

Program shortcut

Application shortcut

Document shortcut

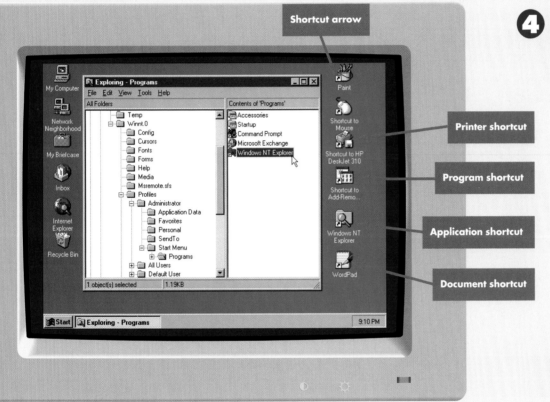

5 To remove a shortcut from the desktop, right-click the short-cut. Then select Delete from the context menu. Alternatively, you can simply drag the shortcut onto the Recycle Bin.

6 To rename a shortcut, select the icon, press F2, then type in the new name. (Alternatively, you can right-click the shortcut and choose Rename.)

How to Launch Applications at Startup

You probably work with the same group of applications day in and day out. Rather than launching these applications during each working session, you can add them to the Windows NT Startup folder on the Start menu. That way, Windows NT 4 launches the applications for you automatically when you log on. Here's the easiest way to do this.

▶ **1** Click the Start button and choose Settings, then Taskbar.

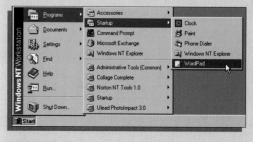

7 To make sure it worked, click the Start button, then Programs. The Startup menu should now contain the application you just added (in this case, WordPad).

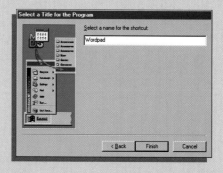

6 Type in the name of the shortcut here. Then press Finish.

2 Now you'll see a window called Taskbar Properties. Click the Start Menu Programs tab in it.

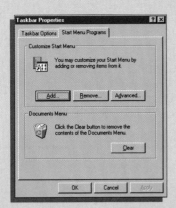

3 To add programs to the Startup group, click the Add button. Doing so opens a window called Create Shortcut. It's the first in a series of screens that walks you through the process of adding applications to the Startup folder. (Notice that this window is called Create Shortcut. That's because you won't actually be moving applications to the Startup folder, but rather adding application shortcuts to it.)

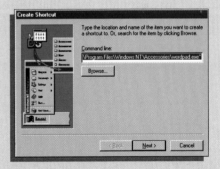

4 In the command line, you must enter the entire path name of the program you want to add to the Startup folder. The easiest way to do this is to press the Browse button, which lets you scan the Windows NT Explorer. Once you've found the file you're looking for, double-click it and Windows NT 4 automatically enters the path name in the command line. Click Next.

5 Now, click the Startup folder and press Next. This opens a window called Select a Title for the Program.

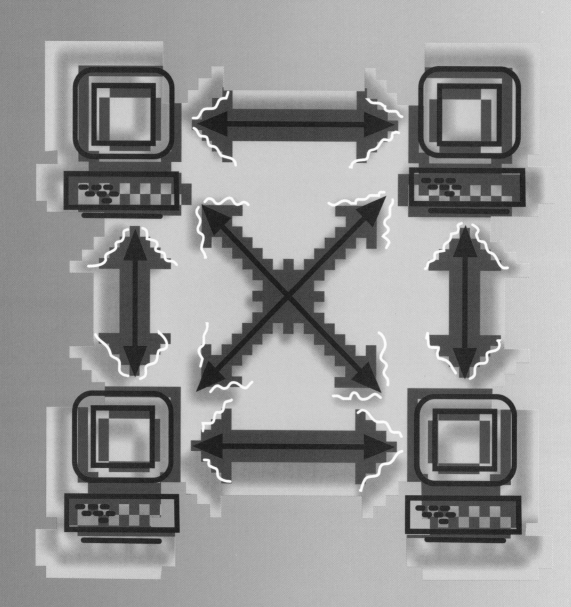

CHAPTER 4

Working with Folders and Files

 Organizing files is key to successfully managing your desktop. If you've worked with previous versions of Windows, such as Windows 3.1 or Windows NT 3.51, then you're accustomed to performing such tasks as viewing, moving, copying, and deleting files and folders using the Program Manager and the File Manager. If you're a former DOS user, you did all this by typing DIR, MOVE, COPY, and ERASE at the command line. However, with Windows NT, you perform these and other file management tasks using a single tool: the Windows NT Explorer. Explorer provides a hierarchical, or outline, view of all your folders and files. For example, click once on any folder in the Windows Explorer, and you'll see a list of its contents (or subfolders).

Using the Windows NT Explorer, you can do everything you did with earlier versions of Windows and then some. For example, Windows NT doesn't limit the length of a file name to eight characters, but lets you assign long file names to both files and folders. A long file name can contain up to 255 characters and can even include spaces. (The only characters you can't include are forward and back slashes (/ and \), colons (:), asterisks (*), angled brackets (< and >), and a vertical rule (|). The advantage of long file names is that they let you name files and folders more intuitively, by using names that more accurately reflect their contents.

In this chapter, you'll learn everything you need to manage the desktop efficiently: creating, deleting, viewing, moving, copying, and finding files and folders.

How to Use NT Explorer

When you open the NT Explorer, it displays a window with two panes. The left one contains a hierarchical list of *all* folders on the current disk. The right pane, which is also called the *content window*, displays everything within the selected folder—documents, programs, and other folders. There are lots of different ways to view and manipulate these items. You can copy and move files from one folder to another, or delete them altogether.

▶ **1** To open the Explorer, click the Start button, Programs, and then Windows NT Explorer.

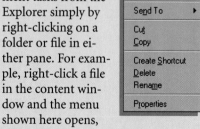

6 You can perform many file management tasks from the Explorer simply by right-clicking on a folder or file in either pane. For example, right-click a file in the content window and the menu shown here opens, allowing you to open, print, rename, or delete a file. (See "How to Copy and Move Files and Folders" later in this chapter to learn how to use the other options on this menu.)

TIP SHEET

▶ The Explorer contains a toolbar with icons for managing files, but it isn't on screen initially. To add this toolbar to the Explorer window, open the View menu, then select Toolbar so that a check mark appears beside it. The toolbar then appears across the top of the Explorer window. It contains icons you can click on to cut, copy, paste, and delete files, as well as icons for changing the way files appear in the NT Explorer window (see "How to View Files or Folders" later in this chapter).

▶ To reverse the last file operation you performed, open the Edit menu and select the Undo command. This is an easy way to correct file and folder mishaps, such as moving a file to the wrong folder or accidentally deleting a file.

2 The Explorer window that opens is command-central for managing files. In the left pane, select the folder whose contents you want to view. Beside each folder you'll notice a plus (+) or minus (–) sign, which you click on to expand (+) or collapse (–) the folder's contents. (Only folders that contain subfolders have a + or – beside them. If only files are in the folder, you won't see a + or – sign.)

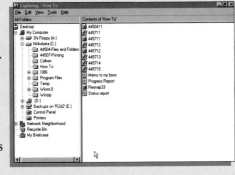

3 To open a folder and view its contents, click the folder in the left pane. In response, the Explorer displays all the folder's files in the right pane, or content window. To resize each pane, position your cursor precisely over the line dividing the Explorer screen. When it's properly positioned, the cursor changes to a two-headed arrow—like you see in this screen—you can drag right or left, depending on which pane you want to enlarge.

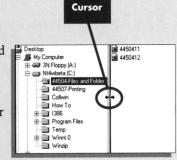

Cursor

Left pane

Right pane, or Content window

NT Explorer toolbar

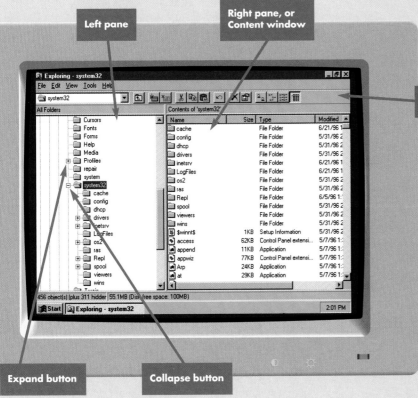

Expand button

Collapse button

5 To open a document, double-click its icon in the content window. In the screen above, for example, double-clicking on the memo pad icon that identifies a WordPad document will open the document called Status report.

4 You can also customize the way in which you view items in the content window by opening the View menu. For example, you can arrange icons in alphabetical order by file name, by file type, by size (from smallest to largest), and by date (starting with the most recently accessed file on the top of the list).

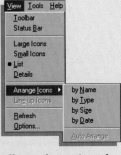

How to Create and Delete Files and Folders

U sing the NT Explorer you can create new folders and files on your hard disk, floppy disk, or other media. As you'll see, creating files and folders is easy; the trick lies in organizing them in an intuitive way, so it's easy to find files when you need them. If organization isn't your strong point, you're in luck: NT Workstation 4 includes a Find utility for quickly locating lost files and folders.

1 To create a new folder in NT Explorer, first select the source—that is, the disk or folder—where you want to place this new item.

TIP SHEET

► **To rename a folder, press the F2 key, then start typing. Like files, folders can have names up to 255 characters in length. If the folder name is very long, you'll have to stretch the Explorer pane to view it in its entirety.**

► **To create a shortcut to a folder, use the right mouse button to drag the folder to another location. When you release the right mouse button, a menu pops up with the option Create Shortcut(s) Here. Click it.**

► **You can select multiple files simultaneously using one of two methods. If all the files you want to delete are adjacent, select the first one in the list, press the Shift key, then click the last document in the series. However, if all the files you want to delete are not adjacent, select the first one, then press Ctrl and hold it down while you select the rest of the documents for deletion.**

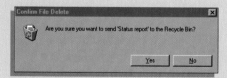

6 Windows NT doesn't automatically delete files and folders; instead, it sends them to the Recycle Bin, where you can recover these items if you decide you don't want to delete them. (See Chapter 2 for more information on working with the Recycle Bin.)

2 Now pull down the Explorer's File menu, choose New, and then Folder. Then look in the right Explorer pane: At the very bottom, you'll see a folder icon and beside it a label that reads New Folder.

File	Edit	View	Tools	Help
New ▶		Folder		
		Shortcut		
Create Shortcut				
Delete		Briefcase		
Rename		Bitmap Image		
Properties		WordPad Document		
		Rich Text Document		
Close		Text Document		
		Wave Sound		
		WinZip File		

📁 Collwin
📁 Exchange
📁 Found.000
📁 How To Use NT ...
📁 New Folder
📁 Program Files

3 To rename the folder, start typing immediately. As you start typing, you overwrite the "New Folder" label. After typing the new folder name, press Enter.

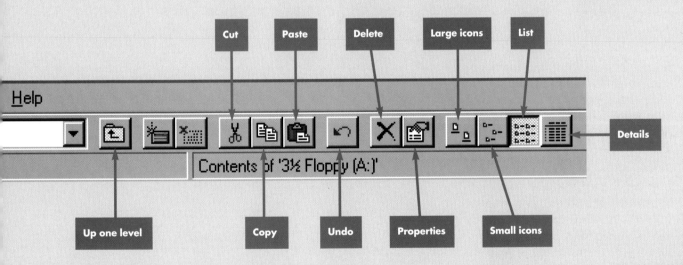

Cut | Paste | Delete | Large icons | List

Help

Contents of '3½ Floppy (A:)'

Details

Up one level | Copy | Undo | Properties | Small icons

4 Alternatively, you can create new folders right on the desktop, without ever opening the NT Explorer. Just position the cursor on a blank spot of the desktop and press the right mouse button. Choose Folder from the menu that appears. (A new folder appears. To rename it, follow the same procedure you used in step 3 above.)

Arrange Icons ▶
Line up Icons

Paste
Paste Shortcut
Undo Delete

New ▶ | Folder
Properties | Shortcut

Briefcase
Bitmap Image
WordPad Document
Rich Text Document
Text Document
Wave Sound
WinZip File

5 Deleting a folder or file is just as easy as creating one. Open NT Explorer, select the file or folder you want to delete, press the right mouse button, and then click Delete.

Open
Print
Quick View

Send To ▶

Cut
Copy

Create Shortcut
Delete
Rename

Properties

How to View Files or Folders

U sing the View menu, you can change the way the folders and files in the Explorer's right pane—or content window—appear. For example, you can enlarge or reduce the icons that represent them, list each item in the folder, and even view details such as the file type (whether it's a WordPad document, for example), the file size, and the date it was last modified.

▶ **1** To change the way in which you're viewing folders, open the View menu. Using this menu, you can choose Large Icons shown in the monitor.

TIP SHEET

▶ **To create a shortcut to any file, right-click it and while pressing the right mouse button drag the file to the place you want the shortcut to appear (say, in another folder or on the desktop). A menu then appears. Choose the item called Create Shortcut(s) Here.**

▶ **NT Workstation 4 maintains a lot of information about files and folders. To view it, right-click a document in the right pane, choose Properties, then the Statistics tab. It contains information such as the dates on which the file was created, last modified, and last accessed. It also tells you how many times the document has been revised, so you can track the number of drafts. (If you like, on the Summary tab you can even enter comments, such as who requested the changes you made to each draft.)**

▶ **The status bar at the bottom of the NT Explorer displays the number of objects in the selected folder, as well as the size of the object, and the amount of free disk space remaining on your hard disk. To hide this bar, open NT Explorer's View menu, then click on Status Bar so that the check mark disappears.**

6 While working in NT Explorer, you might want to switch to an application, such as WordPad, and create a new file. When you switch back to NT Explorer, you won't see this new file, so you'll have to update the view. To do this, open the View menu, then choose Refresh.

2 If a folder has a lot of files, however, you might want to choose Small Icons instead.

3 To view more details about each item in the folder, choose List from the View menu. Selecting Details from the View menu enhances the list by adding information, such as the file type, the file size, and the date you last modified the file.

Large icon view

4 Regardless of whether you display files as icons or in a list, you can reorder them by choosing Arrange Icons from the View menu. Doing so automatically rearranges icons the way you choose: alphabetically, by name; by file type (thus grouping all WordPad documents, for instance); by size (from smallest to largest); or by date (with the newest ones on top).

5 You can also decide which file extensions appear in the NT Explorer. To do this, open the folder you want to look at. From the View menu, click Options first, and then the View tab. To see files with any extensions, choose Show all files. To prevent files of certain extensions from appearing in NT Explorer, choose the extensions in the list box and select Hide files of these types. (File extensions are three-character identifiers that indicate what application was used to create a document. If you create a file using NotePad, for example, it will have a .TXT extension. All file extensions begin with a period.)

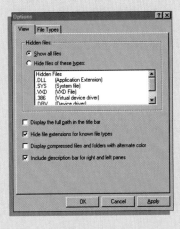

How to Copy and Move Files and Folders

Although copying and moving files and folders is a basic operation, there are a surprising number of ways to do it. The method you use often depends on whether the destination is on the same disk or a different one. It also depends on the Explorer view you're using. Here, we'll show you the easiest method and when to use the alternatives.

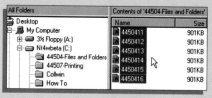

▶ **1** To copy files or folders to another location, first open the NT Explorer and select the items you want to copy.

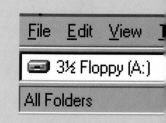

▶ Another way to delete files is to press the Delete key on your keyboard with the file highlighted.

▶ If you want to copy or move a file but you can't see the source and target folder on screen at the same time, here's an easy workaround. Select the source file, then choose Copy or Cut from the Edit menu. Then move to the destination folder, choose Edit again, then select the Paste command.

▶ You can select multiple files simultaneously using one of two methods. If all the files you want to copy or move are adjacent, select the first one, press Shift, then click the last file in the series. However, if all the files are not adjacent, select the first one, then press Ctrl and hold it down while you select the rest of the documents.

5 When you release the right mouse button, a menu appears. Choose Copy (or Cut). Then highlight the destination folder, press the right mouse button, and choose Paste.

2 To *copy* one or multiple files to a destination on the same disk (from one folder on the C: drive to another, for instance), select them, then press and hold the Ctrl key while using your mouse to drag the files to their destination. The original files remain in the source folder, and a copy of each appears at the destination. To *move* files to a destination on the same disk, just drag them to the new location. The original files no longer appear in the source folder.

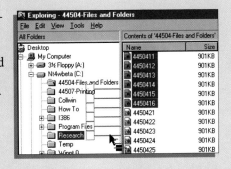

3 If you moved files when you intended only to copy them, pull down the NT Explorer's Edit menu and select Undo. (Or click the Undo icon from the Explorer's toolbar.)

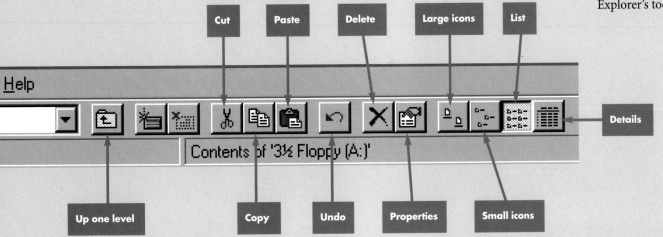

Cut | Paste | Delete | Large icons | List

Help

Contents of '3½ Floppy (A:)'

Details

Up one level | Copy | Undo | Properties | Small icons

4 An easy way to select objects you want to move or copy is to draw a rectangle around a group of files and folders. To do this, place the cursor above (and a little to the left) of the first file you want to move. Now press the right mouse button and, keeping it pressed, drag the cursor until you have drawn a rectangle around the rest of the files. All the files you've "lassoed" should be highlighted, which is your cue that they've been selected.

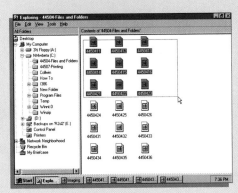

How to Find a File or Folder

No matter how organized you are, misplacing files is inevitable. Fortunately, Windows NT 4 includes a Find utility for searching for files and folders by name, by location, or even by the text it contains. If your computer's attached to a network, the Find tool can help locate other computers.

 1 Click on the Start button, then choose Find. Doing so displays a secondary menu with the two entries you see here. To search for a file or folder, click the first item on the menu.

Now you should
see the Find All
Files dialog box on
the screen. In the
Named box, type
all or part of the
file's name. In the
Look In box, enter
the drive where you think the file resides. When you're
done, click the Find Now button.

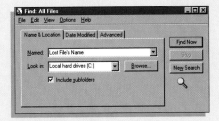

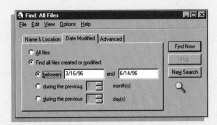

3 If you're unsure of the file's name,
then try searching for it by date.
To do this, click the Date Modified
tab, where you can instruct the
Find utility to search by specific
date criteria. When you're done,
click the Find Now button.

4 Another way to search is to type
text that the file contains, such as a
word or phrase. To do this, click
the Advanced tab and type in the
text. (See the Tip Sheet for details
on how to refine text searches.)

5 No matter what type of
search you perform, the
search results are dis-
played in a window that
appears right below the
search dialog box. To see
if a document in this window is indeed the one
you were after, double-
click its icon and NT 4
opens the file for you.

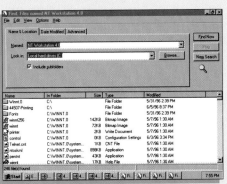

CHAPTER 5

Using Floppy and Hard Disks

Computers are widely used as instruments for manipulating data. When data is not being used (or sometimes, even when it is) it is stored on disks. There are two types of disks: floppy disks and hard disks. Floppy disks are removable, inexpensive, and small and light enough to fit into your shirt pocket. However, they don't store a lot of information (1.44MB max). The other type, the hard disk, is a device that is inside your computer. Hard disks are much larger, heavier, and more expensive than floppy disks. They are usually not removable and can store hundreds or thousands of times the information that a floppy can. Which kind you use depends on what you are doing, but one thing is certain—you can't use Windows NT without them.

In this chapter, you'll learn how to work with disks, including how to view the contents of a disk, format one, check it for errors, and see what disk drives are available to Windows NT.

How to See What Disks Are Attached to Your Computer

Depending on the configuration of your computer, you'll have several disk drives connected to it. You may have access to a floppy disk, a local hard disk, CD-ROM drives, removable media drives, and network drives. My Computer, which is typically located in the upper-left corner of the Windows NT desktop, displays icons representing all the disks you can use with your computer. Each drive is also represented by a letter. Typically, the floppy drive is A:, the hard disk is C:, and the CD-ROM is D:.

▶ ❶ Double Click the My Computer icon.

TIP SHEET

▶ You can change the My Computer display by using the View option in the menu bar. This allows you to select large icons (the default), small icons, a list view, or detailed information about a drive.

▶ You can also change the order in which the drives are displayed. By default, they are listed in descending order according to drive letter. To change this, click View from the My Computer menu bar, and place the cursor over Arrange Icons. This opens another menu with options you can use to display by drive letter, type, size, or by the amount of free space on each one.

2 This opens a window showing all of the disks available to your computer. Each type is represented by a different icon, as shown here.

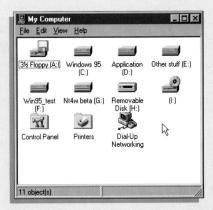

3 Some disks (for example, network drives that you're not logged in to) might have a red "X" through them. This means that those drives are not currently available to you.

4 Other icons, like the floppy disk icon, look the same whether or not there is a disk inserted into the drive. If you click one of these icons when no disk is present, you receive an error message. To avoid this, insert the disk before clicking its icon.

How to View the Contents of a Disk

The first step to working with a disk is to find out what files it contains. Once you know what files are stored on a disk, you will be able to decide what to do with those files (see Chapter 4, "Working with Files and Folders"). The place to go for this information is the My Computer icon on your desktop.

▶ **1** Place the mouse cursor over the My Computer icon, located on the Windows NT Desktop (usually in the upper left), and double-click.

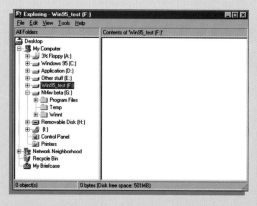

5 The procedure is identical for other types of disks. From the Explorer window, you can view the contents of any other disk in the left pane. (If you're looking at the contents of a floppy or other removable disk, make sure the disk is in the correct drive before double-clicking it, or you'll get an error message.)

2 This brings up the My Computer window. It contains graphical representations, or icons, of all of the disks on your computer including floppy disks, hard disks, CD-ROM drives, and network drives. You'll also see folders for the Windows NT Control Panel, Printers, and an icon to initiate Dial-Up Networking.

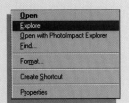

3 You'll notice that each disk is assigned a letter, and in some cases a label. Right-click on the disk you want more information about. (For this example we'll choose one of the hard drives in the system, drive G.) Then choose Explore from the menu that opens.

Folder icon

4 A Windows NT Explorer window lists all the disks in the left pane, with the contents of the one you selected expanded one level. The folders and files on the disk you selected are displayed in the right pane, or content window. Folders are represented by a yellow folder icon, while files are depicted by either the file's particular icon, or in some cases, a generic file icon. Double-clicking one of the folders will update the window to display the contents of the folder you selected.

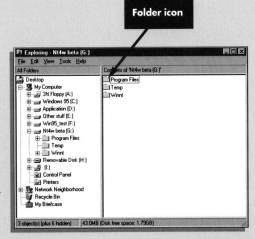

How to Format a Disk

Before you can save data to a disk, it must undergo a process called *formatting*. Formatting sets up the disk in a way that makes it possible to store and retrieve data. Whether the disk you are formatting is a floppy or a hard disk, the process is the same. However, formatting should always be done with care. If any data already exists on a disk, formatting can destroy it. You will probably format floppy disks or other removable disks most often. Formatting hard disks is also possible, but generally not advisable, because it can render your system unusable. In this example, a $3^{1}/_{2}$ inch floppy disk is formatted.

► **1** Double-click the My Computer icon, located in the upper-left corner of the Windows NT desktop.

TIP SHEET

► Before you format a disk, make sure that it is not open in My Computer or Explorer. If it is, you won't be able to format it.

► If you want to format a hard disk, you can choose between two file systems, FAT (File Allocation Table) and NTFS (New Technology File System). Choosing NTFS will give you more options when formatting the disk. If you choose NTFS, you'll also be able to select Allocation Unit Size. This refers to the size of the chunks that Windows NT uses to store data. The default is 4,096 bytes, but you will be able to choose 512, 1,024, or 2,048 bytes. If you store a lot of large files, you should choose a larger Allocation Unit Size.

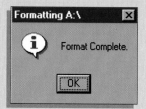

7 When formatting is finished, a window pops up to notify you that the process is complete. Click OK. The disk is now ready to use.

2 Select the icon that represents the disk you want to format. Place the mouse cursor over it, and right-click. Choose Format from the resulting menu. The Format window will appear.

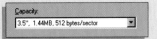

3 First choose the capacity you want. You should format the disk to the highest capacity possible, unless you will need to use the disk in a drive that doesn't support that capacity. For 3½ inch floppy disks, the default is 1.44MB.

4 You can give the disk a label to help you identify it. Type it into the space provided. The label can be up to eleven characters long, including spaces.

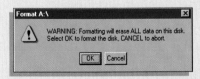

6 When you're ready, click Start. You'll receive a message warning you that existing data will be destroyed. If you don't need the data, click OK. You'll be able to see the status of the format process by watching the status bar at the bottom of the window.

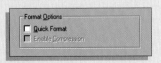

5 If you're formatting a disk that's been previously formatted, you can select Quick Format to save time. This will format the disk much more quickly than normal, but the end result is the same.

How to Check a Disk for Errors

From time to time, errors can occur on floppy or hard disks. These errors can damage or destroy your data and can range from minor to catastrophic. Fortunately, Windows NT can detect and correct many disk errors. For example, if you have trouble accessing a file on a disk you'll want to use NT tools to check your disks for errors. It's also a good idea to check your disks for errors periodically, just as a precautionary measure.

▶ **1** Double-click the My Computer icon, which is located on the Windows NT desktop, usually in the upper left-hand corner.

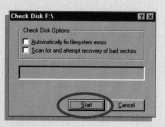

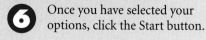

6 Once you have selected your options, click the Start button.

2 This brings up the My Computer window, which shows all of the disks that are connected to your computer. Right-click the disk you want to check for errors, and then select Properties from the resulting menu.

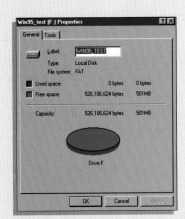

3 You are now looking at the Properties sheet for the disk you selected, with the General tab highlighted. Click on the Tools tab.

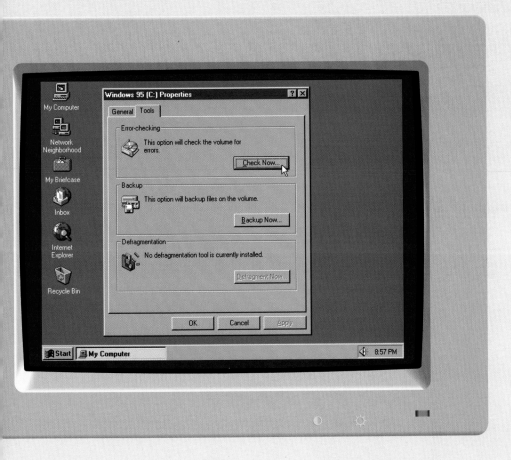

4 Click on the Check Now button in the Error Checking section of the Tools tab.

5 Before the error-checking process starts, you can specify two options. First, you can tell Windows NT to automatically repair any disk errors it finds. Second, you can have it scan for bad sectors and try to move the data within them to a safer location.

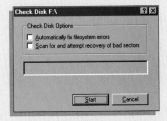

How to Compress a Disk

At some point, you may run out of hard disk space. When this happens, there are two choices—buy a new hard disk, which can be expensive and a hassle to install, or compress your existing disk. Compression changes the way data is stored on a disk so that more information can exist in the same amount of space. When you need to use a file, NT automatically decompresses it back into its original form. When the data is no longer in use, it is recompressed and stored. In most cases, you can almost double the effective storage capacity of your hard drive by enabling compression. There is one drawback, though. You can only compress disks that have been formatted with the NTFS file system.

▶ **1** Double-click the My Computer icon, which is located on the Windows NT desktop, usually in the upper left-hand corner.

TIP SHEET

▶ At any time, you can uncompress a disk by removing the check mark from the disk's Properties sheet. Before you do, make sure that the disk has enough capacity to hold all of your data in uncompressed form. For example, if you compress a 250MB disk to hold 500MB of data, you won't be able to uncompress the disk because the amount of data on the compressed disk exceeds the original capacity.

2 This brings up the My Computer window, which shows all of the disks that are connected to your computer. Right-click the disk you want to compress, and then select Properties from the resulting menu.

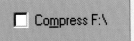

3 If the disk you selected was formatted by NTFS (NT File System) and is capable of compression, you'll see an empty box labeled "Compress <*drive letter*>" in the lower left corner of the disk's Properties sheet. Click it so that a check mark shows up in the box. Then click the Apply button.

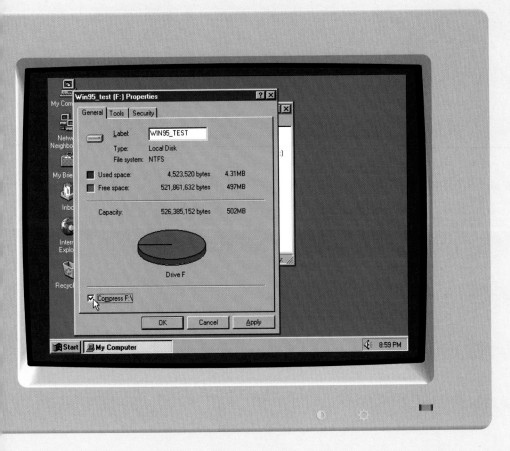

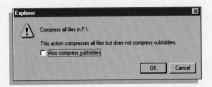

4 If you also want to compress subfolders, click the check box. Compressing subfolders will give you a bit more space. Click OK.

5 You'll see a status window showing the progress of the compression process. Depending on how large your hard disk is, compression can take several minutes or even hours. Unfortunately, NT doesn't indicate how long compression will take.

CHAPTER 6

How to Use Windows NT's Built-in Applications

Windows NT 4 comes with several built in applications, ranging from productivity tools to utilities and games. WordPad is a no-frills word processor that provides basic text formatting features. Although it lacks the features and power of premiere word processors such as Microsoft Word, Corel WordPerfect, and Lotus WordPro, WordPad can get the job done. Similarly, Paint, Windows NT 4's built-in drawing program, comes with basic tools of the trade for creating freehand drawings and diagrams with preformed objects, such as flowcharts. Those of you upgrading from earlier versions of Windows will notice one big difference, though: Unlike its predecessor, Paintbrush, Paint lets you save pictures in only the bitmap (.BMP) format and *not* in the much more compact .PCX format. (Although .PCX format requires less hard-disk space, it only allows the display of up to 256 colors, while .BMPs support up to 16 million colors.)

Windows NT also comes with the handy CD Player for playing audio CDs in your CD-ROM drive. For example, you can easily set the CD Player to play specific tracks in random order. Finally, if you're the gaming sort, check out Windows NT's games. You'll have to install them separately, though, using the Add/Remove applet you learned in Chapter 3, "Working With Applications," because they don't install automatically when you first load Windows NT onto your computer.

How to Use WordPad

Windows NT comes with a built-in word processor called WordPad. It's nowhere near as powerful as full-featured word processors like Microsoft Word, Lotus WordPro, and Corel WordPerfect, but it can certainly handle basic word processing and formatting tasks.

▶ **1** To open WordPad, click on the Start button. Then choose Programs, Accessories, and WordPad. The program launches and presents you with a new, empty document.

▶ To copy or cut text and paste it in a new location, you can use the **Ctrl+C** (copy), **Ctrl+X** (cut), and **Ctrl+V** (paste) keys instead of the menu commands. You can also ust the Cut, Copy, and Paste buttons on the toolbar to perform these operations.

▶ Two other ways to reverse operations are by pressing the Undo icon on the toolbar or by pressing **Ctrl+Z**.

▶ To hide or reveal WordPad's toolbar, Format bar, ruler, or Status bar deselect the item from the View menu so that there's no check mark beside it.

▶ Besides WordPad, Windows NT includes a text editor called NotePad. It's for reading, editing, and creating files containing *only* text—that is, letters of the alphabet (upper- and lowercase), numerals 0 through 9, and symbols such as the pound (#), at (@), and asterisk (*) signs. It's useful for editing HTML files.

7 To undo any action—application of color or formatting attributes, a move operation, color, whatever—choose Undo from the Edit menu.

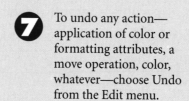

6 To color text, highlight it and then click the Format bar's Color icon. Applying color is useful for drawing attention to parts of an e-mail message. And if you have a color printer, you can color text for use on paper as well as on screen.

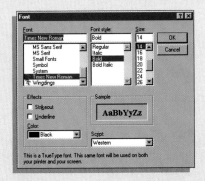

2 You can apply text attributes—such as boldface, italics, or underlining—to your document. To do this, first use the cursor to highlight the text you wish to format and then select the attribute you want to apply from either the Format bar or the Format menu's Font dialog box.

3 To move a portion of text, first use the cursor to highlight it. Then, while pressing the left mouse button, drag the text to its new location (during the drag operation a small square attaches to the cursor). Or, move text by selecting it, pressing the right mouse button, then choosing Cut from the menu that opens. Then move to the new location for the text and choose Paste from the same menu.

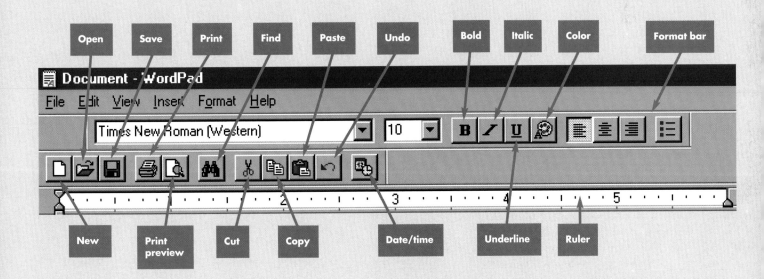

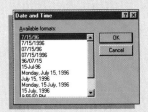

5 To enter the current date or time into a document, position the cursor where you want the date or time to appear. Then click on the toolbar's Date and Time icon, choose the format you like, and click OK.

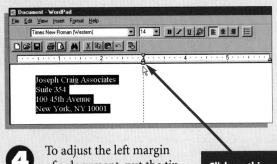

4 To adjust the left margin of a document, put the tip of the cursor on the small box on the ruler and drag it to the setting you want.

Click on this marker and drag to set the margin.

How to Use Paint

Paint is a built-in Windows NT program you can use to draw, edit, and view pictures. You can even create drawings that combine graphics with text, or embed a drawing in another file, such as a WordPad document. One caveat, though: Paint saves files in the bitmap, or .BMP format only. As a result, you can use it to view only .BMP files and not graphics in other file formats, such as .PCX and .GIF. Nonetheless, for basic drawing tasks it fits the bill.

1 To open Paint, click the Start button, then choose Programs, Accessories, and Paint.

7 Along the bottom of the screen is the *palette*, which you use to change the color of text or shapes, and the canvas background or foreground.

TIP SHEET

▸ **To wipe the canvas clean, press Ctrl+Shift+N.**

▸ **To reverse a Paint command, open the Edit menu and select the Undo command. It can undo the last three operations you performed.**

▸ **To repeat an effect, such as a brushstroke, choose Repeat from the Edit menu, or press F4.**

2 On the left side of the drawing area is a toolbox containing media tools, which are shown below. The brush, pencil, and spray can tools are designed to produce effects similar to the real McCoy. There are icons for creating shapes (rectangles, circles, ovals, and lines) and for entering text and erasing. To use a tool, just click on it. Then move the cursor to the empty drawing area, or canvas, and start drawing while holding down the left mouse button.

3 Below the toolbox is an *options box* that displays the various settings for the tool you select. Click the brush, for example, and you'll see different shapes and widths the brush can produce. Or, click the line tool to see the different widths of lines you can create with it.

Options box

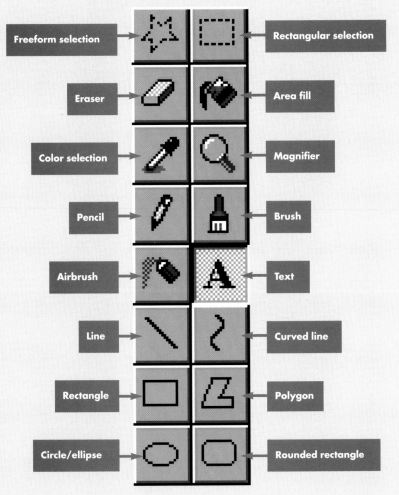

Freeform selection

Rectangular selection

Eraser

Area fill

Color selection

Magnifier

Pencil

Brush

Airbrush

Text

Line

Curved line

Rectangle

Polygon

Circle/ellipse

Rounded rectangle

4 To add text to pictures, click the text tool. Then create a text frame by dragging the cursor diagonally to create a text box. Then open the View menu and select the Text toolbar, from which you can choose the font, point size, and attributes (boldface, italics, or underline).

6 Now click the right mouse button and choose Copy (or Cut) from the menu. Place the cursor where you want the objects to appear, press the right mouse button, then choose Paste. The objects appear in the new location.

5 You can't drag and drop objects you've drawn from one part of the screen to another. But you can copy or move them. To do this, choose the rectangular selection tool from the toolbox. Then drag the cursor diagonally across the area until you've enclosed the objects you want to copy or move within a dotted rectangle.

How to Use the Calculator

Windows NT 4 has a powerful built-in calculator that can operate in two modes: Standards or Scientific. In Standard mode, it functions as a simple pocket calculator, handling basic operations such as addition, subtraction, multiplication, and division. In Scientific mode, the calculator can perform statistical calulations (such as finding the mean of a series of numbers) and scientific functions (such as finding sines and cosines).

▶ **1** To open the Calculator, first click on the Start button. Then choose Programs, Accessories, then Calculator.

TIP SHEET

▸ **To enter numbers using your numeric keypad rather than the mouse, just press the Num Lock button.**

▸ **Another way to open the View menu is by pressing Alt+V.**

▸ **The Scientific calculator has a button labeled Exp for entering numbers in scientific notation.**

▸ **To change the sign of a number from positive to negative (or vice versa), click the +/- button.**

What's This?

6 For help on any calculator button—Standard or Scientific—right click it. Then choose "What's This?" from the menu that opens, and a small description window appears. (Aside from a description, this box usually contains keyboard shortcuts to the function, so you can avoid using the mouse.)

2 The calculator has two modes: Scientific and Standard. To switch between them, open the View menu and choose the one you want.

3 To perform simple calculations, enter the first number. The click the plus sign (+) to add, the minus sign (-) to subtract, the asterisk (*) to multiply, and the forward slash (/) to divide. Then type in the next number. Continue doing this until you've entered all required operators. Then click on the equal (=) sign.

4 To perform statistical calculations first click the button on the Scientific calculator labelled Sta. Doing so opens the Statistics box where you type in data. It also activates the Ave (mean value), Sum (sum of the squares), s (standard deviation), and Dat (data entry) buttons.

5 To perform scientific calcuations, first select a number system: hexadecimal, decimal, octal, or binary. Then click on an operator (such as log or exp). Type in the next number. When you've entered all required operators and numbers, click the equal sign.

How to Play Games

Windows NT 4 comes with several built in games: Freecell, Minesweeper, Pinball, and a new version of an old favorite, Solitaire. To install one or all of these games, you've got to use the Control Panel's Add/Remove Programs applet. You'll learn to install games here; learning to win them is up to you, though.

▶ **1** Click the Start button, Settings, then Control Panel.

8 Now click on the Start button. Under Programs, Accessories, Games, you'll see Freecell, Minesweeper, Pinball, and Solitaire.

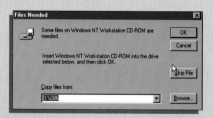

7 The Files Needed dialog box then appears. In the Copy files from field, type in the drive containing the file Windows NT needs: D:\i386. Windows NT then retrieves the files it needs and copies them to your hard disk.

TIP SHEET

▶ Just above the Description area of the Games window is an indication of the amount of space a game requires as well as the free space available on your hard disk.

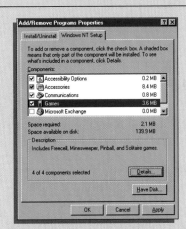

2 Double-click the Add/Remove Programs icon. Doing so opens the Add/Remove Programs Properties dialog box.

3 Click on the Windows NT Setup tab. In the Components section, select Games.

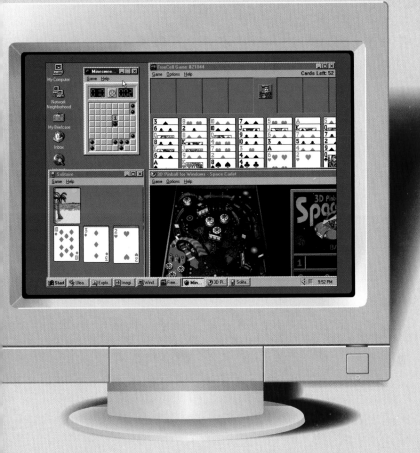

4 Now click the Details button to open the Games window, which lists the four games Windows NT comes with. Highlight a game and a brief synopsis of it appears in the Description area. Now *deselect* the games you don't want to install. Then click OK to return to the Windows NT Setup tab.

5 Now click the OK button on the Windows NT Setup tab.

6 Next, the Insert Disk window prompts you to insert the disk containing the files you want to install. Insert the Windows NT CD in your CD-ROM drive. Click OK.

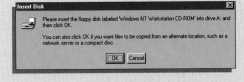

How to Play Audio CDs

Windows Windows NT has a utility, the CD Player, that you can use to play compact disks on the CD-ROM drive connected to your computer. Pop a compact disk in the CD-ROM drive, close it, and it starts playing. Here's how to use the CD Player, plus some tips on getting the most out of it.

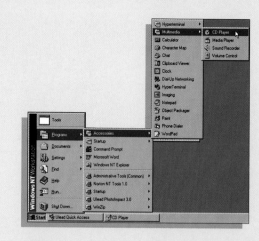

▶ **1** To start the CD Player, click on the Start button, then choose Programs, Accessories, Multimedia, and CD Player. Now insert a compact disk in the CD-ROM drive.

TIP SHEET

▶ **To adjust the volume, right-click the speaker icon in the Taskbar's Tray and select Open Volume Controls from the menu that opens. Now adjust the slider under CD Audio until the volume is as you like it.**

▶ **If the toolbar isn't visible when you open CD Player, select Toolbar on the View menu.**

6 To customize the CD Player, open the Options menu and select Preferences. Among other settings, you can determine whether the CD continues playing when you exit the CD Player (deselect "Stop CD playing on exit") and the amount of time you want to elapse between tracks ("Intro play length").

2 The CD Player window appears on your desktop. Click the Play button to begin playing the audio CD. Even if you minimize the CD Player, the music continues to play.

3 If you like, you can create a play list specifying which CD tracks to play; this lets you skip songs you don't like. To create a play list, on the Disc menu select Edit Play List. The Disc Settings window opens.

Track time elapsed

Track time remaining

Disc time remaining

Random track order

Edit play list

Intro play

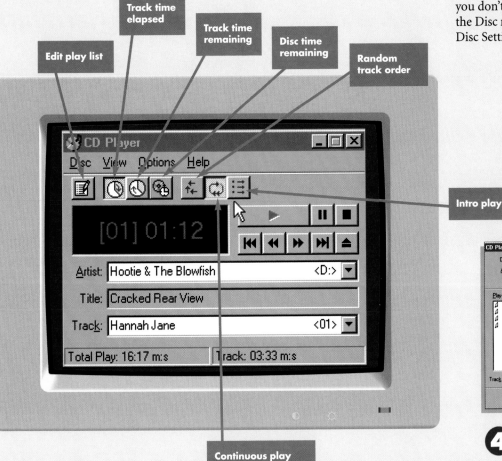

Continuous play

4 Enter the artist's name and the title of the CD in the appropriate fields. The Available Tracks box lists all the songs on the CD currently in your CD-ROM drive. To change the order in which tracks play, first select Clear All to erase all items in the play list. Then choose the track you want to play first (here, it's Track 5, "Time"). Press Add. Now, in the Track 05 field, enter the song's name. Then press Set Name. Repeat these steps until the play list is complete. Then click OK.

5 Now open the CD Player, choose the artist you want to listen to from the Artist drop-down list, then press the Play button. Tracks play in the order you have specified.

CHAPTER 7

Printing Documents

 If you thought that choosing the Print command was all there was to printing, you're in for a surprise. Windows NT gives you as much control over printing as you want. For example, you can print one or more documents simultaneously from the Windows NT Explorer. Or, create a printer shortcut and drag documents directly onto it for speedy printing. You can even control documents after you've clicked the Print command, by opening the printing queue and resuming, restarting, or cancelling print jobs. In this chapter, you'll learn how to do all this, and find useful tips to help you work faster and smarter.

You'll also find out how to install a printer. In most cases, this is a snap, because Windows NT provides a "Wizard," which is a series of screens that ask questions and literally walk you through the install process.

One caveat, though: If you're upgrading to Windows NT from an earlier version of Windows—NT 3.51, Windows 3.1, even Windows 95—your old printer driver won't work under NT Workstation 4. Fortunately, NT 4 ships with a generous supply of new drivers, and it most likely includes one for your printer. If your driver is not on the Windows NT CD, you'll need to find out when an NT 4 driver will be available. You can do this either by calling the printer manufacturer directly or by surfing to a World Wide Web site that tracks drivers, such as the Windows Sources DriverFinder at www.wsources.com.

How to Install a Printer

To get a printer up and running, you have to install special software called a *driver*. It acts as a translator between the operating system and the hardware, telling the printer how to interpret fonts and page layout instructions, among other things.

In most cases, you'll only need to install a printer once. But there may be times when you need to connect to another printer: when your regular printer isn't working, for instance, or when you want to use the new color laser down the hall. Here's the easiest way to do this under Windows NT.

▶ **In step 4, you selected your printer from the manufacturers list. If your printer's not on the list, click the Have Disk button. This opens a dialog box that tells you to insert a disk containing the driver for your printer, which should have come with your printer. If you don't have the disk, either call the manufacturer or surf to their Web site, where most printer manufacturers post their latest drivers.**

▶ **In step 6, notice that the Share name on the screen reads *CanonBub*, rather than Canon Bubble Jet BJC-610, as it originally appeared. Why did NT 4.0 truncate the name to eight characters? Because users running older operating systems (DOS and Windows 3.x) that don't support long filenames wouldn't recognize the longer version, and would thus be unable to print.**

▶ **1** Click the Start button and position your cursor over Settings, which automatically opens another menu containing three items: Control Panel, Printers, and Taskbar. Click the Printers folder.

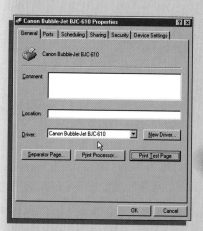

8 If you opted for a test page, NT 4 asks whether it printed correctly. If it did, the printer's Properties sheet opens. Here, you can enter information, such as which department is using the printer (and who to call when it needs toner). Click OK, and you're done.

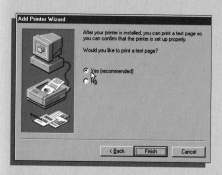

7 The next dialog box asks if you want to print a test page. Click Yes—it's the only way to make sure the printer is installed correctly. Then click Finish. At this point, you'll be prompted to insert the NT 4 CD, which contains the printer driver.

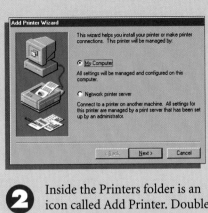

2 Inside the Printers folder is an icon called Add Printer. Double click it and the Add Printer Wizard opens. Because you're installing a printer connected directly to your PC, choose My Computer.

3 Place a check mark beside the port the printer is connected to. Most printers use the computer's parallel port, which is usually LPT1.

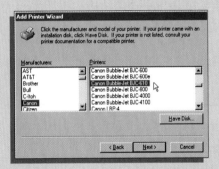

4 Now, choose the printer manufacturer and model. The left pane contains an alphabetical listing of dozens of manufacturers. Click yours. Then, in the right pane, you'll see a list of specific models.

5 After selecting your model, the printer's name automatically appears. You can rename it whatever you like, though.

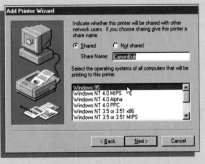

6 If you don't want to share the printer, skip this step. If you do want to share this printer with other users on your network, click Shared and type in the name you want to use to identify the printer. For example, you might name the printer down the hall "Hall Printer." Now, select all the operating systems running on all the computers that will be using this printer.

How to Print a Document

No matter what Windows application you're printing from, the steps are the same. You launch the application you used to create the document, open the file you want to print, and choose the Print command from the program's File menu. In Windows NT 4, however, you can speed printing by creating a shortcut icon to your printer and dragging any document to it, regardless of whether the document is a text file written in Notepad or a graphic presentation developed in PowerPoint. Here's how to do it.

TIP SHEET

▶ **To print several documents at once, open the Windows NT Explorer and find the folder containing the files you want to print. Select all the files you want to print and, with the files highlighted, press the right mouse button. Then choose Print from the context menu that opens. Windows NT 4 automatically opens the application you used to create the documents, then loads, prints, and closes first the documents, and then the application.**

▶ **There are two ways to select several files at once for printing. The method you use depends on the order in which the files appear. For example, if all the files you want to print are adjacent, select the first one in the list, press the Shift key, then click the last document in the series. However, if all the files you want to print are not adjacent, select the first one, then press the Ctrl key and hold it down while you select the other documents you want to print.**

▶ **To edit the label that appears below the printer shortcut you just created, select the icon. Then press the F2 key on your keyboard; a frame appears around the icon's label. Now make your changes and press Enter.**

▶ **1** Click the Start button, Settings, and then Printers.

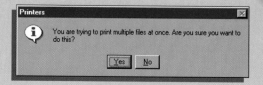

6 If you're printing several documents at once, NT 4 asks whether you really want to print them all.

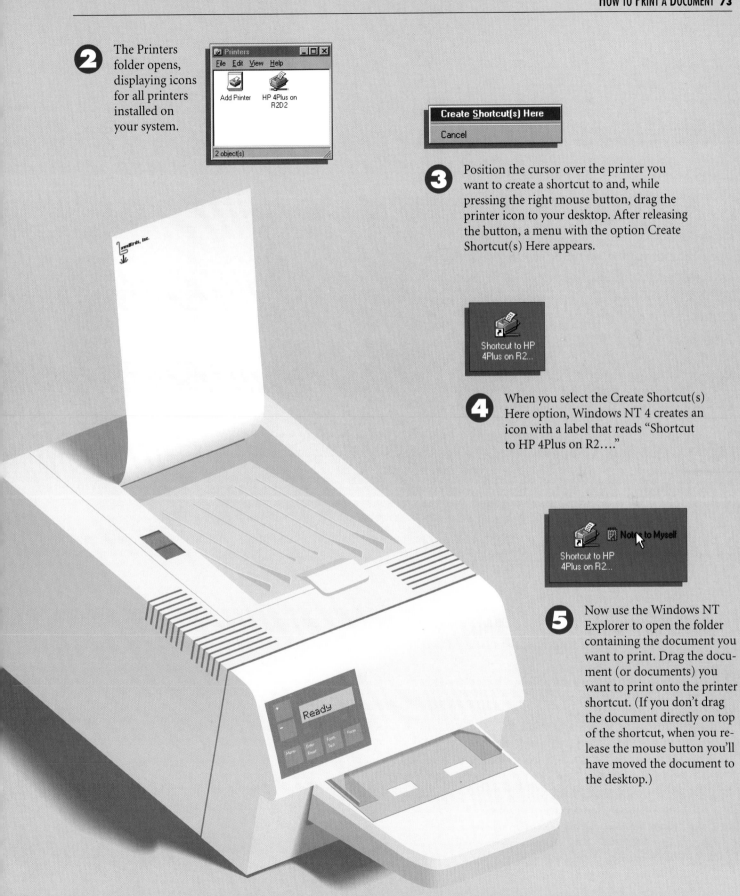

2 The Printers folder opens, displaying icons for all printers installed on your system.

Printers
File Edit View Help

Add Printer   HP 4Plus on
              R2D2

2 object(s)

Create Shortcut(s) Here
Cancel

3 Position the cursor over the printer you want to create a shortcut to and, while pressing the right mouse button, drag the printer icon to your desktop. After releasing the button, a menu with the option Create Shortcut(s) Here appears.

Shortcut to HP
4Plus on R2...

4 When you select the Create Shortcut(s) Here option, Windows NT 4 creates an icon with a label that reads "Shortcut to HP 4Plus on R2...."

Shortcut to HP
4Plus on R2...

5 Now use the Windows NT Explorer to open the folder containing the document you want to print. Drag the document (or documents) you want to print onto the printer shortcut. (If you don't drag the document directly on top of the shortcut, when you release the mouse button you'll have moved the document to the desktop.)

How to Manage the Print Queue

A print queue is a list of all documents waiting to be printed. To view all documents in the queue, simply double-click the printer shortcut you just created. Doing so opens a window that displays not only the documents' names, but the status of the various print jobs, who's printing them, and the number of pages in each document. From here, you can cancel a print job altogether, or just pause the print job temporarily.

▶ **1** Position the cursor over the printer shortcut icon, and then press the right mouse button. A menu appears. Choose the item called Pause Printing (when you do, a check appears beside it). Choosing this option delays printing until all documents you want to print are in the queue.

TIP SHEET

▶ Another way to view documents in a print queue is by double-clicking the printer in the Printers folder, which is off the Start button, under Settings.

▶ To quickly check the status of your printer, right-click the printer icon in the Taskbar. It will tell you whether the printer is active or inactive, for example.

▶ Your printer may not stop printing immediately after you pause a print job. It all depends on the type of printer you're using. For example, laser jet printers, such as the Hewlett-Packard LaserJet series, continue to print for a minute or so because they have lots of memory in which they store the document. Inkjet printers, which have much less memory, stop printing the moment you click Pause Printing.

5 To cancel a print job, select the document in the print queue, click the right mouse button, and choose Cancel. When you do, that document name disappears, and it won't print.

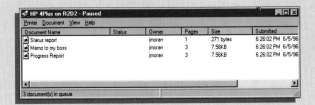

2 Double-click the printer shortcut icon and you'll see a list of the names of all documents in the print queue.

3 To change the status of one or more jobs in the queue, first select the document or documents, and then press the right mouse button. You'll see a menu with several options, including Pause, Resume, and Restart. Click Pause to temporarily suspend printing. (Restart begins printing a document all over again; Resume picks up where it left off.)

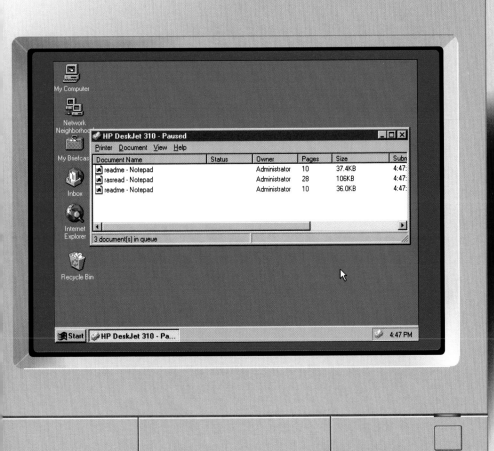

4 To resume printing the other documents—that is, those that you haven't paused—open the Printer menu and click on the Pause Printing option. When you do, the check beside it disappears, and the other jobs continue printing.

What to Do If You Have Trouble Printing

Although installing and using your printer seems (and usually is) a straightforward process, problems can and do occur. For example, you might be unable to print any documents, or, if you can print, documents might look different on paper than they did on the screen. Or, printing may just be unusually slow. Windows NT 4 includes a help system that actually asks questions on the type of problem you're having, and then suggests ways to fix it based on your response.

1 Click the Start button, then Help, and the Help Topics window appears.

5 Another common problem is that printing is very slow. Again, Windows NT tries to pin down the exact problem, this time by asking if it took a long time for the document to come out of the printer, or whether you couldn't use your application for other tasks while the job was printing.

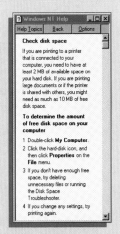

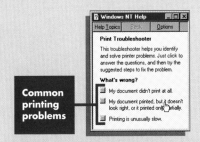

Common printing problems

2 Double-click the item under Troubleshooting called "If you have trouble printing," and select the box that describes the print problem you're having.

3 One of the most common problems is that documents won't print. If this occurs, you'll be asked if you printed a test page after installing your printer, which you should have done (see "Installing a Printer" earlier in this chapter), so click Yes. If the document still won't print, the problem could be a shortage of space on your hard disk. Windows NT 4 tells you how to check the amount of disk space available.

4 If the document printed but it looks funny on paper, check the second option ("My document printed, but it doesn't look right, or it printed only partially.") You're then prompted to answer a series of questions on the exact nature of the problem. Check the one that matches the problem you're having.

CHAPTER 8

Using a Modem

 If you want to use the Internet or a commercial online service such as America Online (AOL) or CompuServe, then you'll need to install and setup a modem. Before getting started, however, it's important to understand a few things about modems. First, they come in internal and external models: We recommend you use an external modem. It's easier to install—just plug one end of the cable into the modem and the other into the serial port on the back of your computer. External modems also have lights to indicate the status of your connection (to learn what these lights mean, see the Tip Sheet in "How to Install a Modem").

More important than the model, however, is the modem's speed. Today's fastest modems can send and receive data at 33.6 Kbps (or 33,600 bits per second), which is the fastest speed possible over ordinary telephone lines. Although this may sound impressive, even at this speed many World Wide Web sites and online services may take a while to display—particularly those containing lots of graphics and photos.

In this chapter, you'll learn how to install a modem, set up the Inbox that comes with Windows NT so you can send and receive e-mail, use HyperTerminal to access bulletin board services (BBSs), and use your computer to place ordinary telephone calls. You'll also find troubleshooting tips in case you have problems using your modem.

How to Install a Modem

The first step is to connect the modem to your computer. If you're using an external modem, plug one end of the cable into the modem and the other end into a free serial port on the back of your computer. (The serial port usually has a nine-pin connector labeled COM1 or COM2.) If you're using an internal modem, you must shut down and unplug your computer, remove the case, and slide the modem into an empty slot. Make sure the modem's settings don't conflict with other hardware installed in your system.

1 Click the Start button, then choose Settings, and Control Panel.

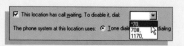

8 If you have call waiting, you may want to disable it before using your modem so that online sessions aren't interrupted by incoming telephone calls. To do this, check the box for disabling call waiting, and then select the code your system uses (usually *70) from the drop-down menu beside it. (If you're not sure which code to select, call the local phone company.) Click OK to close the Dialing Properties, and then click Close to shut the Modem Properties window.

7 The next step is to tell Windows NT how to dial. For example, you may need to dial 9 to access an outside line (which is usually the case in most offices).

TIP SHEET

▶ **If you use a calling card, select the option called Dial using Calling Card in the Dialing Properties dialog box. Then click the Change button and choose your calling card from the list that appears. If your card is not in the list, you can create an entry for it by pressing the Change button and then choosing New.**

▶ **External modems are better than internal models because they provide at a glance information about the status of a connection. For example, most modems include these indicators: SD (sending data); RD (receiving data); CD (carrier detect), which means your modem is connected to another modem); and OH (off hook), which indicates that the modem is using the line.**

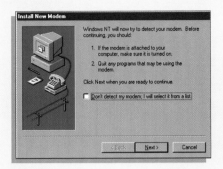

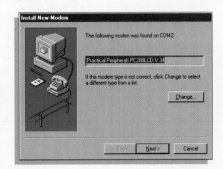

2 Double-click the icon labeled Modems to open the Install New Modem wizard. (Wizards are Windows NT tools that walk you through a particular process, such as setting up modems). Windows NT can automatically detect most modems, so *don't* put a check beside the option you see on the screen. Click the Next button to start installing your modem.

3 If Windows NT recognizes the modem, you'll see its name and location on the screen. Here, for example, the modem name is Practical Peripherals PC288LCD V.34 and it's installed on the serial port named COM2. Click Next.

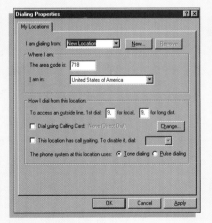

4 Windows NT will then set up your modem and let you know whether the process has been successful. If it's gone smoothly, click Finish to open the Modems Properties dialog box.

5 To customize the way your modem places calls, click on the Dialing Properties button. Doing so opens a dialog box— with a tab called My Location—in which you enter information about the location you're calling from.

6 In the field labeled "I am dialing from," type in the name of the city. Next, enter the area code from which you're dialing, and then choose the country from the drop-down menu.

How to Set Up the Inbox

The Windows NT Inbox icon represents a built-in application called Windows Messaging System, which provides the operating system with its e-mail capabilities. Using it, you can exchange e-mail over the Internet. One caveat, though: Setting up the Inbox is only half the job. To actually use it to send and receive e-mail over the Internet, you must have an account with an Internet Service Provider (ISP). The Tip Sheet tells you how to find one.

▶ **1** Click the Start button, then choose Settings, and Control Panel.

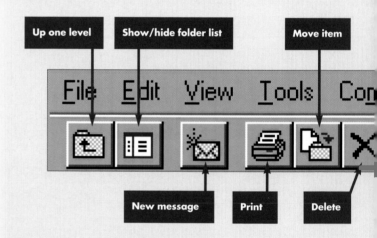

TIP SHEET

▶ If you don't have an ISP, find a friend who does and surf to a site with information on ISPs, such as thelist.com. This site contains a list of Internet Service Providers. If you're on a corporate network that provides Internet access, you won't need to find your own ISP. Instead, check with your LAN administrator, who'll provide the information you must enter in the the Microsoft Exchange Setup wizard.

6 When you double-click the Inbox icon, the Windows messaging Setup Wizard opens. Deselect Microsoft Mail and press Next. The Wizard then asks a series of questions you must answer to send mail over the Internet. (To complete the Wizard, you'll need some information from your ISP, if you're not on a network, and from your LAN administrator, if you are on a network.

2 Double-click the Control Panel's Add/Remove Programs icon, which opens the Add/Remove Programs Properties dialog box. Now select the Windows NT Setup tab, and then click the Microsoft Exchange item.

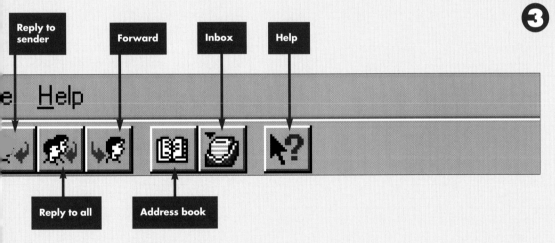

3 Click the Details button, which displays the three components you see in this screen. Deselect Microsoft Mail, because the only options you need to work with are Internet Mail and Microsoft Exchange. Then click OK, which returns you to the original Windows NT Setup dialog box. Click OK again to begin setting up the Inbox.

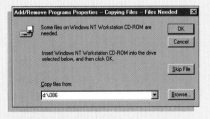

4 Windows NT now asks you for the Windows NT CD. Insert it, and in the field labeled "Copy files from," type **d:\i386** if your CD-ROM is the d: drive and you're using a PC based on an Intel chip (that is, a 486 or a Pentium). Click OK.

5 Windows NT now copies the files it needs to the computer's hard disk, which takes about one minute. When it's done, an Inbox icon should appear on the desktop. Like all Windows NT applets, the Inbox has its own toolbar, which is shown above.

How to Send and Receive E-Mail

The Inbox lets you exchange e-mail with friends and colleagues around the corner or around the world who are also using the Internet. Keep in mind, though, that the Inbox cannot gather the mail you receive from online services such as AOL and CompuServe. For example, if you're an AOL user and another AOL member sends you a message, it won't appear in the Windows NT Inbox. The same goes for CompuServe. To get your mail, you'll have to log on to each service and check the inbox that each one provides.

▶ **1** Double-click the Inbox icon on the desktop. Doing so opens the Windows NT Inbox.

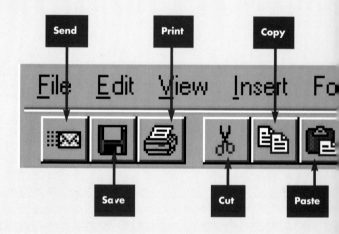

▶ **A quick way to begin a new message is by pressing Ctrl+N, which opens the Inbox.**

▶ **To select a recipient from the Address Book, click on the To: or cc: buttons in the New Message Window.**

▶ **In the Business tab, you can view only one phone number at a time. If a contact has multiple phone numbers—say for beepers, cellular phones, pagers, and so forth—click on the Phone Numbers tab, which has entries for these and many other numbers.**

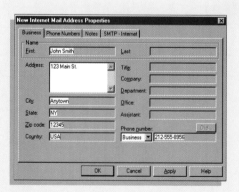

7 Click on the Business tab. Here, you can enter information on business and personal contacts.

2 To send mail, pull down the Compose menu and choose New Message. (Or, click the New Message icon on the Inbox's toolbar, which is shown below.)

3 In the New Message window that appears, type the address of the recipient in the To: field, add the addresses of anyone you wish to cc:, and type your message. Then pull down the File menu and click the toolbar's Send button. (The enlarged toolbar to the left identifies the other buttons.)

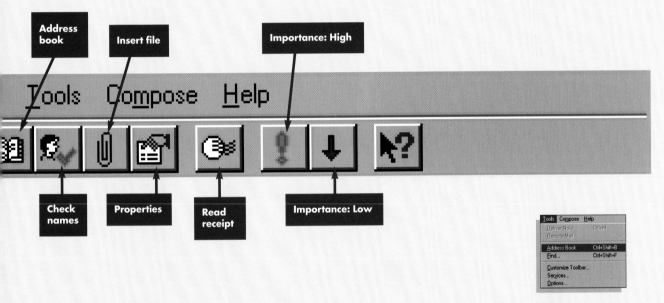

4 If you regularly correspond with a recipient, you should add their name to the Inbox's address book. This way you don't have to continually type in their name and address. To add names to the Address book, pull down the Tools menu, then choose Address Book.

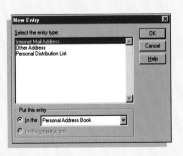

5 Click the first icon on the Address Book's toolbar, which looks like a small white Rolodex card. Doing so opens a New Entry window, where you select the type of address. In this case, it's an Internet Mail Address, so choose that. Now click OK.

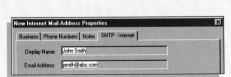

6 The SMTP-Internet tab appears first. Relax. It looks more intimidating than it actually is. In the Display Name field, simply type the name of the person you wish to enter in the Address Book. In Email Address, type in their Internet address.

How to Use Phone Dialer

Windows NT includes a utility called Phone Dialer that you can use to dial any phone number. It's especially helpful if your telephone doesn't have a speed dial feature to let you dial a number by pressing just one button. In fact, Phone Dialer lets you create up to eight speed dial buttons for up to eight people. One prerequisite, though: To use Phone Dialer, you must have already set up your modem.

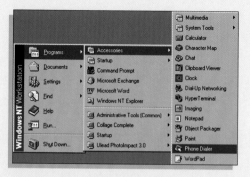

▶ **1** Click the Start button, then choose Programs, Accessories, and then Phone Dialer.

▶ **To dial numbers directly from the Address Book in your Inbox, follow these easy steps. Open the Inbox, from the Tools menu select Address Book, and then double-click the name of the person you want to call. Click the Phone Numbers tab, then press the Dial button beside the number you wish to dial.**

▶ **To create a shortcut to the Phone Dialer, right-click the Start button, then choose Open from the menu that appears. This brings up a Start Menu window containing a Programs folder icon; double-click it. Next, double-click the Accessories folder, which opens a windows containing all Windows NT Accessories, including Phone Dialer. Right-click on the Phone Dialer icon and, while pressing the right mouse button, drag the icon to your desktop. A menu appears; choose Create Shortcut(s) Here and you're done.**

5 You can create speed dial buttons for up to eight people. This lets you dial any one of them with a single mouse click.

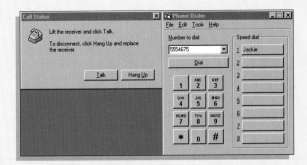

2 To dial a number, use the Phone Dialer's keypad just as you would an ordinary phone. (Or, type the number directly into the blank area below Number to Dial.) Then click the Dial button, and the Call Status window pops open.

3 When the other party answers, click the Talk button (you should have the telephone handset in your hand at this point). To end the conversation, click the Hang Up button.

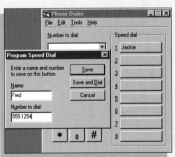

4 To add names to the speed dial buttons, click on a button; a Program Speed Dial window appears. Type the name and number in the space provided. Click Save, or Save and Dial if you want to call the person immediately.

How to Use HyperTerminal

HyperTerminal is a communications application that comes with Windows NT. It's particularly useful for connecting directly to bulletin board systems (BBSs) or to other computers—to transfer files, for example. Although most online communications takes place on the Internet or a commercial online service such as America Online or CompuServe, you may still need to connect to a good old-fashioned BBS now and then.

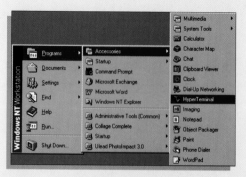

▶ **1** Click the Start button, then choose Programs, Accessories, then HyperTerminal.

TIP SHEET

▶ To change the font in which the BBS text appears, pull down the View menu, then choose Font. A dialog box opens in which you can select the font type and size. There's also a preview window so you can see what a font looks like before applying it.

2 In the Connection Description dialog box, enter the name of the computer you will be connecting to. You can also choose an icon to launch this connection in subsequent sessions. Click OK and the Connect To windows pops open.

3 You'll notice that upon opening, the Connect To window already contains your area code and country—that's because you entered this information when you set up the modem. Now the only information you need to enter is the phone number of the computer you want to connect to. Then press OK and the Connect window opens.

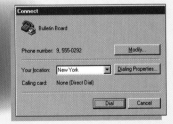

4 Here, press the Dial button. HyperTerminal dials the number for you and waits for a response from the other computer. While placing the call, HyperTerminal pops open a window that displays the status of the call, such as whether it's dialing or has encountered a busy signal. When the remote computer answers, it displays a welcome or log on message.

What to Do If You Have Trouble Using Your Modem

Windows Windows NT makes installing a modem practically foolproof. Still, problems may occur. For example, you may have difficulty installing the modem, or it might not dial a number you've entered in the Address Book. Here, you'll learn how to use Windows NT's online help system to solve these and other common problems.

▶ **1** Click the Start button, then choose Help.

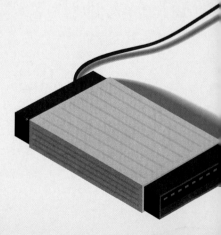

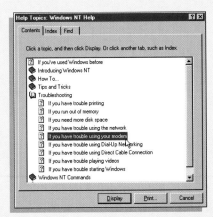

2 Double-click the Troubleshooting item. You'll now see a window with a list of common problems that can occur. Choose the one that reads: If you have trouble using your modem.

3 If your computer isn't dialing properly, click "Dialing doesn't work correctly." Doing so opens a window that narrows the problem even further and suggests solutions. For example, if the modem isn't dialing the number at all, first make sure all the cables are securely connected.

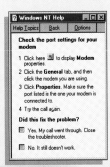

4 If that doesn't solve the problem, click "No, It still doesn't work." Windows NT will then suggest other possible causes. For example, you may have connected the modem to the wrong serial port (COM1 rather than COM2, for instance).

5 Sometimes Windows NT won't be able to solve a problem. If that's the case, Windows NT will recommend that you check your modem's documentation or call the vendor.

TRY IT!

Windows NT comes with software to let you send and receive e-mail across the Internet, as well as browse the ever-expanding World Wide Web. But before you can start doing this, you need a way to connect to the Internet.

If you are on a corporate network, check with your system administrator to see whether your Windows NT machine has Internet access, and, if not, whether you can get it. Another way to access the Internet is by using Dial-Up Networking. Dial-Up Networking is software built in to Windows NT, which lets you connect to the Internet using a modem instead of a network card. Before setting up Dial-Up Networking, you must obtain an account with an Internet service provider (ISP). The ISP will provide you with the information you need to set up Dial-Up Networking, such as the user name, password, and IP address.

Double-click the My Computer icon on the Windows NT desktop.

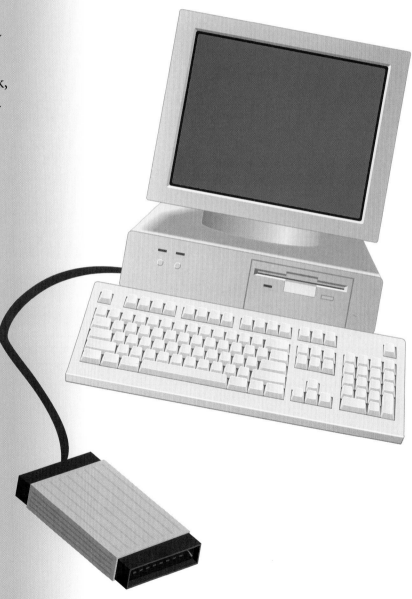

2

The My
Computer
window
will open.
Double-click
the Dial-Up
Networking
icon.

3

A Dial-Up
Networking
window will
appear, offer-
ing some
background
information. Click the Install button to
begin installing Dial-Up Networking.

4

You'll be
prompted to
insert the
Windows NT
CD so that
the Dial-Up Networking files can be copied to
your computer. After you put in the CD, type
the folder name where the files are located
(d:\i386 if your CD-ROM is drive D and
you're running Windows NT on an Intel-
compatible computer) and click OK.
Windows NT will install the Dial-Up Networking software along with various other
networking components it requires.

5

When the
process is
complete, an
Add RAS
Device window will appear in it where you
specify. If you've already installed a modem,
Windows NT should display its name in the
RAS Capable Devices field. If this is the case,
click OK. (If you haven't installed a modem
yet, you can use the Install Modem button to
do so now. See Chapter 8 for more information.)

6

The Remote
Access Setup
window will
appear, listing
the modem
you selected in the previous window.

7

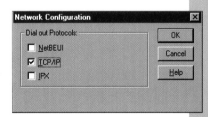

Click the
Network but-
ton. The
Network
Configuration window pops up. Select the dial
out protocol you will be using for your Dial-Up
Networking connection, and click OK. (Your
ISP will be able to tell you which protocol will
be used; usually it's TCP/IP.)

Continue to next page ▶

TRY IT!

Continue
below

 8

 Continue

You're now back at the Remote Access Setup
window. Click the Continue button.

 9

Windows NT
will continue
to set up
Dial-Up
Networking.
When the process is complete, a window
will appear informing you that your
computer needs to be shut down and
restarted for the changes to take effect.
Click the Do Not Restart Button.

 10

Right-click
the Network
Neighbor-
hood icon on
the Windows
NT desktop,
and click Properties from the
resulting menu.

11

The Network
dialog box
will appear.
Click the
Protocols tab.

12

You should
see TCP/IP
displayed in
the Network
Protocols list.
Double-click
it to open the TCP/IP Properties window.

13

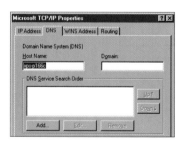

Click the
DNS tab. The
DNS (do-
main name
server) is
provided by
your ISP and lets you locate other computers on
the Internet. Your ISP will have provided you
with one or more DNS addresses. Click the Add
button in the section labeled DNS Service
Search Order.

Type in the
DNS addresses provided to you by your ISP,
then click the Add button. When you're done,
click the OK button at the bottom of the
TCP/IP Properties Window.

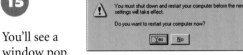

You'll see a
window pop
up informing you that your machine needs
to be restarted. This time, click the Yes button to restart. When Windows NT restarts,
return to the Dial-Up networking icon in
My Computer and double-click it.

A small win-
dow will ap-
pear informing you that your phone
book is empty. That's OK, because you
are going to add an entry now. Click OK
to do so.

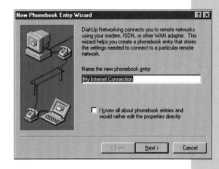

The first
thing to do is
to type in a
name for the
entry. This
can be what-
ever you like,
but it helps
to name it something you'll recognize. After
you've entered a name, click Next to continue.

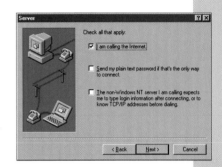

In the next
window,
you'll be
asked to
place a check
mark in the
box next to
any state-
ments that apply to you. For most users, the
first one, "I am calling the Internet," is the
only one that will apply. If you're not sure if
the others apply to you, check with your ISP.
Click Next to continue.

Now, enter
your ISP's
phone num-
ber in the
blank space
provided. To specify one or more alternate
numbers (which NT dials if the primary
number is busy), click the Alternates button. If your ISP didn't provide you with any
alternate numbers, skip to step 21.

Continue to next page ▶

TRY IT!

Continue
below

23

Now it's time
to enter your
user name and
password (pro-
vided to you
by your ISP).
Enter each in the space provided. If you're calling a Windows NT-based server, you'll also need
to specify the domain. Check with your ISP to
see if you need to enter this information. Click
the OK button after entering the information
to initiate the call.

20

Enter the al-
ternate num-
bers one at a
time in the
New phone
number space
and click Add
after each one.
When you're finished, you can adjust their
priority (the order in which they are dialed)
by clicking the Up or Down buttons. When
you're done, click OK.

21

Click the Next button. You've now finished creating a Dial-Up Networking phone book entry.
Click the Finish button.

24

A small dia-
log box will
appear in-
forming you
that the con-
nection is in
progress. When the connection is established,
you'll hear a tone, and a Connection Complete
window will appear. Click OK. Congratulations!
You're on the Net!

22

A Dial-Up
Networking
window ap-
pears, dis-
playing the
name of the connection, the phone number
that will be dialed, and your dialing location.
Click the Dial button.

CHAPTER 9

Surfing the Web

 If you haven't surfed the World Wide Web, you don't know what you're missing. The Web, as it's called, is a complex international network of computers connected over the Internet. What makes the Web special, though, is its use of graphics and its point-and-click interface.

Nowadays, many commercial and non-profit organizations have sites on the World Wide Web. (And those that aren't there yet will be soon.) Some sites offer polished, high-quality information; others publish content of dubious value. This chapter simply shows you how to use the Internet Explorer to get on the Web. The Try It section that follows this chapter, however, does take you to some interesting and valuable sites.

Before continuing, though, take a few moments to familiarize yourself with Web-speak. An *URL*, or universal resource locator, is a fancy name for a Web site's address. Usually, it starts with *www.*, which stands for World Wide Web. Just as you need to know someone's address to visit their house, you must know a Web site's URL to surf to it. Once you've arrived at a site, you'll probably find it's sprinkled with *hyper-links*—text or graphics that bring you to another page when you click on them. You can identify hyperlinks in several ways: When the cursor is placed over a hyperlink, it changes from an arrow to a hand. Also, text hyperlinks are typically highlighted (often in blue) and underlined.

How to Use the Internet Explorer

Windows NT 4 comes with a built-in browser, called Internet Explorer, that you can use to surf the World Wide Web, or the Web, for short. The Internet Explorer's icon appears on the desktop when you install Windows NT. Here, you'll learn the basics of connecting to the Web and using Internet Explorer (IE). One caveat, though: To complete the steps in this chapter, you must already have an account with an Internet service provider or else be able to connect to the Web via your company's local area network.

TIP SHEET

▶ **Multimedia elements on Web pages are slow to download. If you like, you can configure IE so it doesn't display pictures or animations, or play sounds. To do this, from the View menu choose Options. Click the Appearance tab, and deselect the picture, animation, and sound options.**

▶ **To print a Web page, choose Print from the File menu. Or, click the printer icon on IE's toolbar. Remember: If you choose not to show pictures in the Options dialog box, they won't appear When you print the page. All you'll see is a placeholder icon.**

▶ **To search for a word on a Web page and avoid scrolling, from the IE Edit menu click Find. Then type in the word or phrase you want to search for.**

▶ **1** Double-click the Internet Explorer (IE) icon on the desktop. (The graphic shown on the next page identifies all the buttons you'll see on IE's toolbar.)

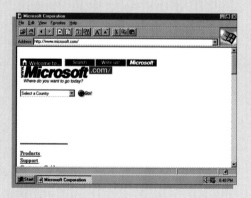

5 Either way, once you're on the World Wide Web and at Microsoft's Web site be patient: The page can take a few seconds to load. (The rate at which a page loads depends on the speed of your modem.) For an in-depth romp around the Internet, see the Try It! following this chapter.

2 The first time you launch Internet Explorer, this Start Page appears. In fact, it will display each and every time you open the browser. (Later in this chapter, though, you'll learn how to replace this plain-vanilla page with one that you choose.)

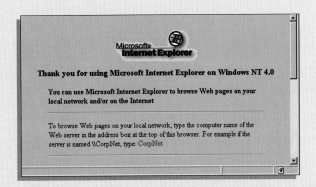

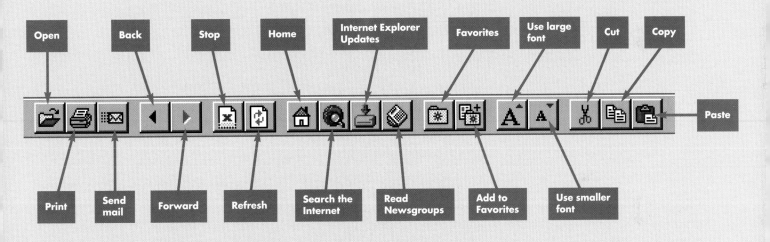

4 If you're accessing the Web through your company's LAN, clicking www.microsoft.com brings you directly to the site. If, however, you're accessing the Web through a dial-up networking connection, clicking www.microsoft.com opens a dialog box that asks if you want to dial a remote network. Click the "Yes, dial" button.

3 Scroll to the bottom of the page until you see the *hyperlink*, shown here, that will take you to Microsoft's Web site. Now click on the link that reads http://www.microsoft.com. (All URLs begin with "http://," but from now on we will omit this prefix when referring to hyperlinks.)

How to Change the Start Page

Internet Explorer lets you select a Start page, which is the page that appears each time you launch IE. The default Start page contains basic information on using Internet Explorer that's useful the first few times you launch IE. But after that, you won't pay it any mind. Why not replace it with a screen that does grab you? For example, if there's a page on the Web that you access frequently, you can have it come up automatically each time you start Internet Explorer—you'll learn how to do that here.

► **1** Double-click the Internet Explorer (IE) icon on the desktop.

TIP SHEET

► If you grow nostalgic for the Internet Explorer's Start page, you can restore it. From the View menu, choose Options, then the Start Page tab. Now press the button called Use Default.

► To see if there's a new version of Internet Explorer, go to Microsoft's Web site at www.microsoft.com. From there, you can download new versions for free.

2 In the Address field, type the URL of the page you want to use as the Start Page.

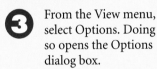

For example, here we're using www.microsoft.com as the Start page. Remember: Although most URLs begin with "http://" (for hypertext transport protocol) you don't need to type all this in when entering an address. Forget about the "http://" and begin typing with the part of the address that reads "www."

3 From the View menu, select Options. Doing so opens the Options dialog box.

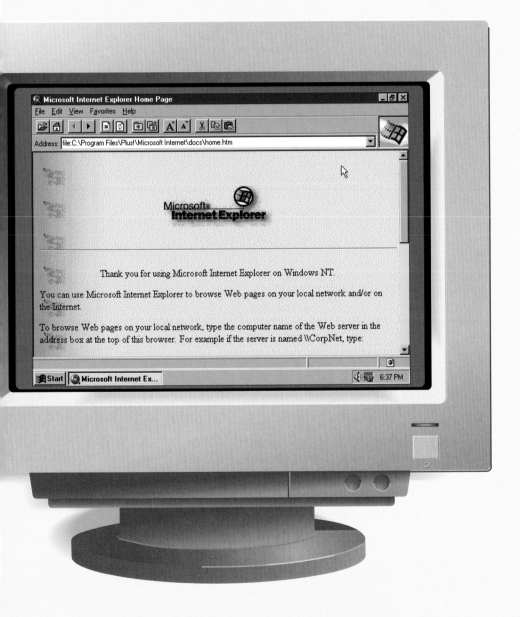

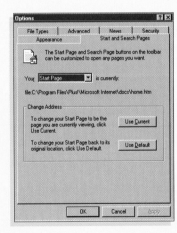

4 Now click the Start and Search Pages tab in the Options dialog box. In the Change Address area, click the button labeled Use Current. This instructs Internet Explorer to automatically load the current Web page each time it launches.

How to Save Favorite Web Sites

Internet Explorer has a feature called Favorites that you can use to save the addresses of the Web sites you visit regularly. This spares you from manually typing in an URL each time you want to surf to a site, letting you access sites easily and quickly.

1 Double-click the Internet Explorer (IE) icon on the desktop.

6 To launch a favorite page, just click on its icon in the Favorites folder.

TIP SHEET

▸ **To add additional Web sites to your Favorites list, repeat steps 2 through 4. You can have as many sites in Favorites as you like.**

▸ **Another way to access a Web site is by typing its URL in the Start menu's Run dialog box.**

2 In the Address field, enter the URL of the Web site you want to add to your Favorites list. Then press Enter to surf to that site.

3 After the page loads, click the Add to Favorites button on the toolbar. Doing so opens the Add to Favorites window.

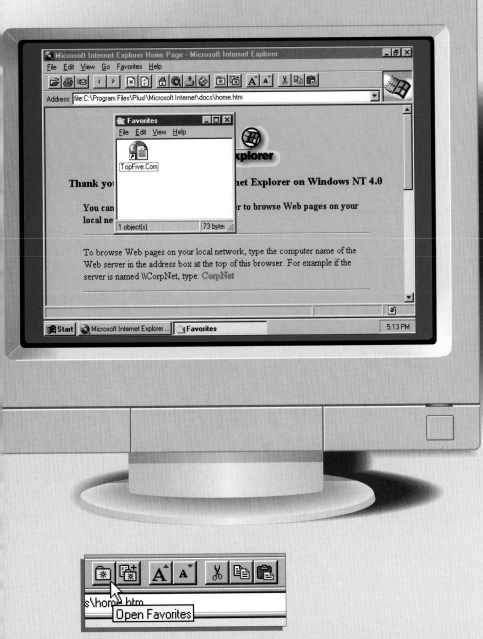

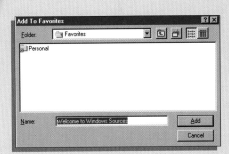

4 When you open the Add to Favorites window, notice that IE has already named the page for you. You can either keep this name or change it by typing in a new one. When you're done, click Add and Internet Explorer adds that Web page to your Favorites folder.

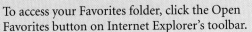

5 To access your Favorites folder, click the Open Favorites button on Internet Explorer's toolbar.

How to Search the Internet

There are millions of Web sites on the Internet and finding the information you need isn't always easy. *Search engines,* such as AltaVista and Yahoo, can help. These tools index or categorize the contents of Web servers and filter information based on search criteria you enter. You can access all of the popular search engines by using the Internet Explorer's Search the Internet tool. Here's how it works.

► ❶ Double-click the Internet Explorer icon. Your Start page loads automatically.

TIP SHEET

▸ For the best results, use boolean operators such as "and" and "or" in your search criteria. They narrow the search so you don't get a million hits. For example, when searching for Windows Sources, we entered "Windows and Sources," which produced 11 hits. However, entering "Windows Sources" yielded over 3 million hits, because Yahoo displays every site containing the word "windows" or "sources." The "and" operator tells the engine to search for both words as one phrase.

▸ To replace the Internet Explorer's search page with another (such as Yahoo or AltaVista), first surf to the search page you want to use. From the View menu choose Options. Next, click on the Start and Search Pages tab, select Search Page from the drop-down menu, and click the Use Current button.

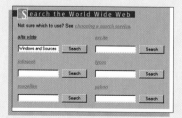

 If you don't find the results you want, try another search engine. Internet Explorer's search page lets you try them all.

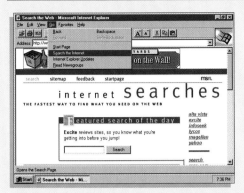

2 To search the Internet, choose Search the Internet from the Go menu. (Or, click on the Search the Internet icon.)

3 Now you'll see the Microsoft Network search page. It contains links to all of the popular search engines and features a different one each time you perform a search.

4 In the blank field, type in the search criteria, then press the Search button. To search for Windows Sources magazine, we entered Windows and Sources (see the Tip Sheet for details).

6 Scroll the window to find the item you want. Then move the cursor over it; the cursor turns into a hand. Now click on the link and you automatically jump to that site.

5 A results window then displays the number of *hits*–that is, the items that matched the search criteria you entered.

How to Play Audio Files on the Web

Many Web sites, including www.pcweek.com and www.msnbc.com, offer more than text and graphics; you can also play audio files. PCWeek, for example, has a feature called PCWeek Radio where you can hear reporters covering computer industry news.

To enjoy audio on the Web, you've got to have a sound card installed. (You need speakers, too, of course.) That's what you'll learn to do here. But before getting started, you must put the sound card into a free expansion slot in your computer, and jot down the resources (such as the IRQ and DMA Channel) that the card uses. Typically, this information is in the documentation or on the sound card itself.

▶ **1** Click the Start button, then Settings, and Control Panel.

8 The System Setting Change window opens; click Restart Now. When Windows NT restarts, your sound card should be working and you can enjoy audio on the Internet.

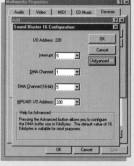

7 In the Sound Blaster 16 Configuration box that appears, you select the Iinterrupt, the DMA Cchannel, and the 16-bit DMA Cchannel, and the MPU401I/O Aaddress. Use the drop- down menus to enter the appropriate values for each. Then click OK. (The options that appear on the pull- down menus vary by card; the ones you see here are for the Sound Blaster 16 card we used.)

TIP SHEET

▶ **To play audio files, most Web sites require you to download a special applet called a *player*. PCWeek, for instance, uses the RealAudio Player.**

2 Double-click the Multimedia icon, which is used to configure devices such as sound cards and CD-ROMS.

3 In the Multimedia Properties window, click the Devices tab— it's the last one on the right.

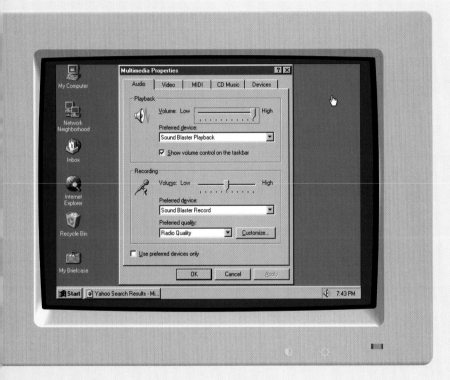

4 Now click the Add button. It lists the multimedia drivers that Windows NT 4 comes with. Find your sound card's name in the list, and double-click it. (If your sound card isn't on the list, click Unlisted or Updated Driver at the top of the list.)

6 Now the fun starts. Because Windows NT 4 doesn't support Plug and Play, you must specifiy what resources the sound card will use. So, in the Sound Blaster Bbase I/O Address, go to the I/O Address area and pick your card's address from the dropdown list. Then click Continue.

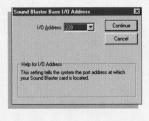

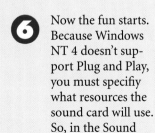

5 The Install Driver window pops up and asks for the Windows NT CD-ROM. (If your device is not on the list, insert the disk that came with your sound card; it contains the driver.) Type in the path (usually d:/i386), and click OK.

ow that you know how to connect to the Internet, it's time to
surf it—and that's exactly what this
exercise will teach you. You'll use the
browser that's built in to Windows
NT — Internet Explorer (IE) — to
navigate the World Wide Web. You'll
also learn how to customize IE to
make the time you spend online
more productive and enjoyable.

Now is a good time to explain *hyperlinks,* which are the mainstay of
the web: A hyperlink is a word, a
group of words, or an image that
you can click on to jump to another page. Typically, text hyperlinks are blue and underlined.
You can also identify hyperlinks
because when the cursor glides
over them, it turns into an
icon of a hand.

1

Double-click
the Internet
Explorer icon on the desktop.

The Internet Explorer Welcome page pops up (unless you've replaced it with another Start page). You're not on the Internet yet, though, since this screen resides on your hard disk.

To get onto the Internet, in the Address field type the address (the URL) of the Web site you want to surf to. For this example, type **www.wsources.com**. Now press Enter. (Internet Explorer automatically inserts http:// so you don't have to.)

It can take a few seconds for the Web page to display. Once it does, move the cursor around the screen; when it changes into a hand, you're over a hyperlink. Click on the hyperlink and you jump to another Web page. Here, we're clicking on DriverFinder.

The next page pops up. Advertisements often appear at the top (and sometimes the bottom) of most Web pages. Typically, these ads are hyperlinks that will take you to the advertiser's Web site.

While IE is locating and downloading the Web page, the clouds in the Windows NT logo move. This indicates that data is being processed. When the clouds stop moving, the data transfer is complete.

Internet Explorer lets you control the way pages appear. For instance, you can enlarge or reduce the font by selecting Fonts from the View menu. When you choose an option, it takes effect immediately.

Continue to next page ▶

TRY IT!

Continue
below

8

IE stores, or caches, Web pages on your hard disk, which speeds page display. The downside is that the page you're viewing may not always be the most recent version. To reload the page and make sure you're viewing the newest version, select Refresh from the View menu. Or press the toolbar's Refresh button.

9

To return to a Web page you viewed previously, click the back arrow on the toolbar. To return to the page you were just on, click the forward arrow.

10

Internet Explorer saves every Web address you enter in the Open field and puts them on its pull-down menu. Open it, select an address, and IE takes you to that site. (IE saves addresses from all sessions, not just the current one.)

11

To print a Web page, select Print from the File menu or click the tool-bar's printer button.

12

Even with a 28.8-Kbps modem, Web pages can take a long time to display, especially those packed with graphics. If you want to cancel a download, click the toolbar's Stop button or select Stop from the View menu.

13

To customize Internet Explorer, choose Options from the View menu.

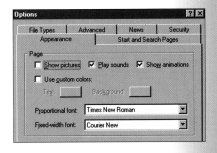

The Appearance tab appears in front. The Page area contains options for controlling the display of pictures, sound, and animation. For example, if you don't want to download graphics, deselect the "Show pictures" option—Web pages download faster without them.

To change the color and underlining of hyperlinks, go to the Shortcuts section. You can control these attributes for links you've already activated, and for those you haven't yet viewed.

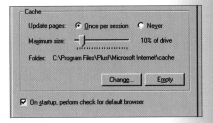

Earlier, you learned that IE caches Web pages. To set the cache size, click the Advanced tab. Then use the Maximum size slider to determine how much of the hard disk the cache should occupy. Larger caches speed the display of Web pages, but consume lots of hard-disk space.

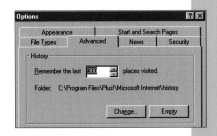

IE saves the addresses of sites you've visited, so you can quickly access them using the back and forward arrows. To set the number of sites you want IE to save, go to the History section and enter a number (300 is the default; 999 is the maximum).

You can copy and paste text and graphics from a Web page to the clipboard. Just click the toolbar's Copy button, switch to the application you want to paste the objects into (we used Paint), then paste it in.

You can save the address of Web sites you want to return to by adding them to a list called Favorites. To do this, while you're on the page select Add to Favorites from the Favorites menu. Or, click the toolbar's Add to Favorites button.

Continue to next page ▶

 TRY IT!

Continue below

 23

A Notepad window containing the source code – that is, the HTML tags – appears.

 20

The Add to Favorites window pops up with the name of the Web site in the Name field. Click the Add button.

 24

There's a button on the toolbar—Internet Explorer Updates—that takes you directly to Microsoft's Internet Explorer home page. Here, you can download the newest version of Internet Explorer.

21

You can then access one of your favorite sites by choosing it from the Favorites menu.

22

Viewing HTML source code is a good way to learn how to design your own Web pages. If you find a Web page you like, select Source from the View menu.

CHAPTER 10

Getting on the Web with Microsoft Peer Web Services

 In Chapter 9, you learned about Internet Explorer, a Web browser that's built into Windows NT 4 and lets you travel to various sites on the Internet. After using Internet Explorer to traverse the Web, you may want to create your *own* Web site for others to visit to learn about your product, service, or yourself.

With Windows NT 4, and some help from an Internet service provider, you can set up your own Internet presence by publishing your own pages on the Web. Microsoft Peer Web Services, which comes with Windows NT 4, can transform your computer into a Web server, allowing you to set up and maintain a Web site of your own.

Setting up a Web site is not for everyone, as it requires considerable time, money, and expertise to get one going. First, you'll need an open connection to the Internet so that others can access your site (an Internet service provider or your phone company are good places to get one). Second, you'll need to learn HTML (Hypertext Markup Language), the programming language with which Web pages are created, and find an application that lets you create HTML documents. Once you've done that, you can use Windows NT 4's Peer Web Services to get yourself out onto the Web. You can also use Peer Web Services to publish information on an *intranet,* which is a network that uses Internet communication standards but is not actually attached to the Internet. In this chapter, you'll learn the basics: how to install Peer Web Services and how to use Microsoft Internet Service Manager, an administration tool.

How to Install Microsoft Peer Web Services

The first step in setting up your Internet presence is to install Microsoft Peer Web Services, which comes with Windows NT Workstation 4. Peer Web Services includes support for three Internet services: World Wide Web, FTP (File Transfer Protocol), and Gopher.

When you install Peer Web Services, Windows NT loads all of the software required to set up and administer your Web site, tying the new Internet components into Windows NT's network infrastructure. The installation also sets up directories into which you can place the files you want to publish and provides a utility you can use to administer your site.

TIP SHEET

▶ **If you don't install all of the components in Peer Web Services the first time, you can go back and add (or remove) additional components by clicking the Start button and selecting Programs, Microsoft Peer Web Services, then Peer Web Services Setup.**

▶ **The complete documentation for Peer Web Services is contained on line in the form of HTML documents viewable with any Web browser (like Internet Explorer). To access them, click the Start button and select Programs, Microsoft Peer Web Services, then Product documentation.**

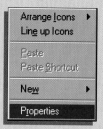

▶ **1** Right-click the Network Neighborhood icon on the Windows NT desktop and select Properties.

8 When Peer Web Services has been completely installed, a window will appear to alert you. Click OK to continue.  The Network Settings Change window will pop up, indicating that you need to restart your computer for the changes to take effect. Click Yes to do so. When Windows NT restarts, Peer Web Services will be ready to run.

7 Next, you'll choose the directories that will contain your online content. There is a separate directory for each Internet service that Windows NT 4 supports: World-Wide Web, FTP (File Transfer Protocol), and Gopher. You can spec-  ify different directories by clicking the Browse buttons. Click OK to continue. (You may get a message asking if you wish to create the directories. If you do, click Yes.)

2 This brings up the Network window. Select the Services tab, then click Add.

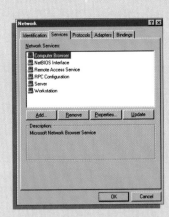

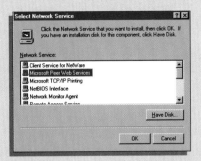

3 The Select Network Service window appears with a list to choose from. Click the Microsoft Peer Web Services item, then click OK.

4 You'll be prompted for the Windows NT CD. Type in the path where the files are located (usually d:\i386), and click OK.

5 Windows NT will load some files, after which the Microsoft Peer Web Services Setup box will appear. Click the OK button to continue. You may see a window informing you that there is no Internet Domain name on your machine. You can create one using the network control panel, by selecting the Protocols tab, then selecting TCP/IP, then DNS, and typing the name into the field labeled "Host Name."

6 Another window will appear where you can select which components of Peer Web Services you want to install, as well as specify the directory where they will reside. Deselect the box labeled "ODBC Drivers & Administration." Click the OK button to continue.

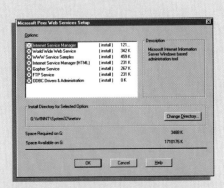

How to Use Internet Service Manager

Now that you've installed Windows NT 4's Peer Web Services, it's time for a quick tour of Internet Service Manager. This utility is a one-stop shop that allows you to control various aspects of your Internet site. For example, you can view the status of the three Internet services that Windows NT 4 supports, and start, stop, or pause any of them. You can also modify the folders in which your documents are published, limit access to any or all of them, and obtain log information detailing activity.

Running Peer Web Services can be pretty complex, so there isn't room here to describe all of the features that Internet Service Manager provides. You'll learn the basics here—then you can go out and explore additional areas on your own.

▶ **1** Click the Start button, select Programs, Microsoft Peer Web Services (Common), and then Internet Service Manager.

6 You can sort the view according to a number of criteria. To do so, select View and then pick one of the options from the resulting menu.

2 The Internet Service Manager appears. This utility lets you administer the three Internet services that Windows NT Workstation 4 supports.

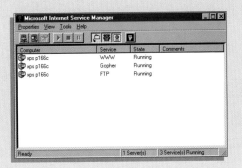

3 You'll see a list containing icons that report the status of all of the Internet services running on your machine (you may also see other machines on the network listed here). To change the properties of a service, click the computer on which the service is running, and select Service Properties from the resulting menu.

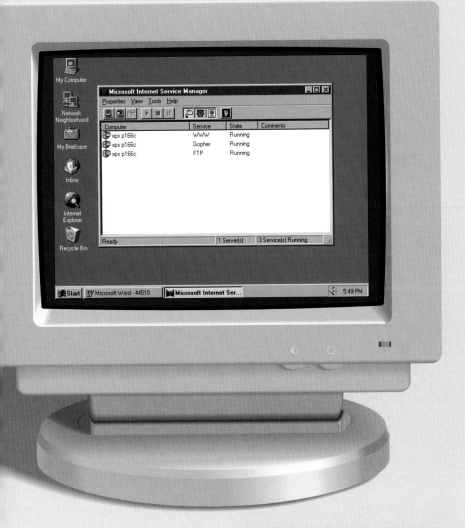

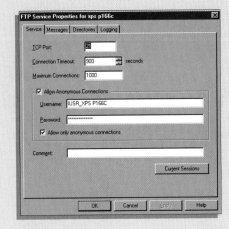

4 The Service Properties window will open. It contains a number of tabs, depending on the service you chose. Here you can control things like the text of system messages, in which directories files will be stored, and what information will be automatically logged. After you've made your selections, click the OK button.

5 You can stop (or pause) a service by right-clicking it and selecting the appropriate menu option. After you've stopped or paused a service, you can restart it by right-clicking it again and selecting Start.

CHAPTER 11

Customizing Windows NT

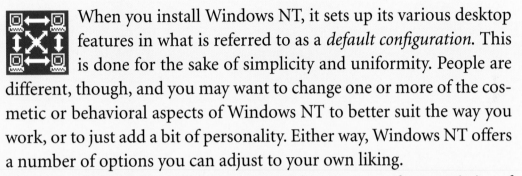When you install Windows NT, it sets up its various desktop features in what is referred to as a *default configuration*. This is done for the sake of simplicity and uniformity. People are different, though, and you may want to change one or more of the cosmetic or behavioral aspects of Windows NT to better suit the way you work, or to just add a bit of personality. Either way, Windows NT offers a number of options you can adjust to your own liking.

In this chapter you will learn how to change many characteristics of Windows NT, such as the screen saver, background wallpaper, mouse settings, date and time settings, Start Menu choice, screen resolution, Taskbar layout, and more.

How to Change the Way Your Mouse Behaves

U sing the mouse is a powerful and easy way to get things done in Windows NT, but unless the mouse works the way you expect it to, using it can be an exercise in frustration. For example, the mouse is automatically set up for right-handed users. Double-clicking an item also proves difficult for some; if so, you can set the mouse so you don't have to double-click quite so fast. Adjusting the mouse settings can make it easier (and more pleasant) to use.

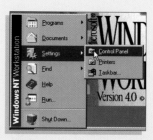

▶ **1** Click the Start button and place the cursor over Settings. Then choose Control Panel from the Settings menu, which will open the Control Panel folder.

TIP SHEET

▶ **If you switch between right- and left-handed mouse operation, it will reverse the role of the left and right mouse buttons.**

▶ **You can use the Pointers tab to change the look of the various mouse cursors you'll see throughout Windows NT. You can also select from a number of pre-defined schemes which will change all of the cursors at once.**

▶ **Use the General tab if you want to connect a different kind of mouse (or other pointing device) to your computer.**

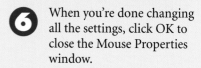

6 When you're done changing all the settings, click OK to close the Mouse Properties window.

2 Look for the Mouse icon and double-click it. This will bring up the Mouse Properties window. The Buttons tab will automatically come up in front.

3 You can select either right- or left-handed operation. If you find that you have trouble starting applications because you double-click too slowly, use the slider bar to adjust the double-click speed and click the box in the test area to see if the new settings work for you.

5 At any time, you can click the Apply button, which will immediately use the new settings without closing the Mouse Properties Window.

4 Click the Motion tab. Here you can adjust the speed at which the mouse cursor travels across the screen. You can also enable the Snap to default option, which will automatically move the mouse cursor to the default button in each window, saving you the trouble.

How to Change the Desktop Wallpaper

Windows NT's plain blue-green background color isn't unpleasant to look at, but just as you would put art on your wall, you might want to add a little flair to your desktop. Adding a pattern or design to the desktop can make your computer better looking and a little more fun to use.

► **1** Click the Start button, place the cursor over Settings, and then click Control Panel.

TIP SHEET

► Another way to open the Display Properties window is to right-click on an empty part of the desktop and then select Properties from the menu.

► You can use the Edit Pattern button to change the default pattern designs Windows NT offers.

► If you have a favorite graphics file in bitmap form, you can use it as wallpaper by clicking Browse from the Background tab and then selecting your file from a disk.

► You can also use the Plus! tab to enhance the look of your desktop and change the desktop icons.

2 Double-click the Display icon. This will bring up the Display Properties window, with the Background tab in front.

3 Choose from the list of patterns on the left and wallpapers on the right. As you click each item, the small monitor in the window will change to reflect the choice you made. If your wallpaper is too small to fill your screen, clicking the Tile option will replicate your wallpaper image until it does.

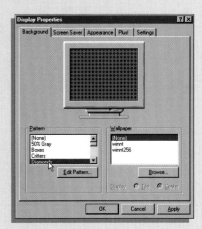

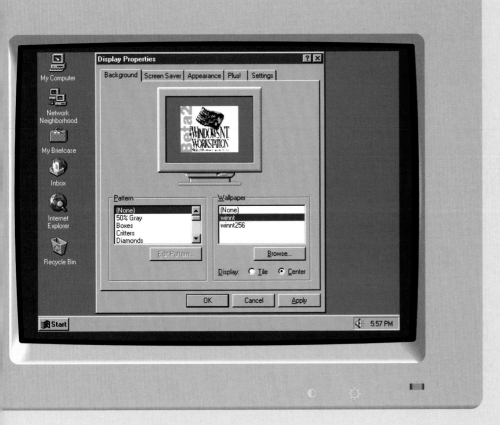

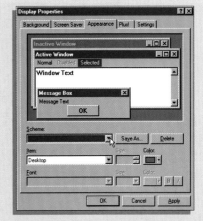

4 Click the Appearance tab. This will let you change the colors of the pop-up windows and menu items. Changes you make here will be reflected in all applications.

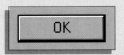

5 When you've finished, clicking OK will confirm your changes and close the Display Properties window.

How to Change the Display Settings

Most computers can display a number of resolutions and color depths. Higher *resolution* means more space on your desktop, and sharper, more defined images. Higher *color depths* let you display more colors on the screen simultaneously, which makes many graphics files, particularly photographs, look better and appear more realistic. The refresh rate, or the frequency at which your screen is updated, can also be adjusted. For example, the default refresh rate is often 60Hz (60 times per second). That may seem like a lot, but it can often result in flicker, leading to eye strain.

 1 Click the Start button, place the cursor over Settings, and then click Control Panel.

TIP SHEET

▸ **To see a list of all of the graphics modes your machine supports, click the List All Modes button.**

▸ **In general, avoid using resolutions higher than 800 by 600 pixels unless you have a large monitor (17 inches or more). Running high resolutions on small monitors can make icons too small to see easily.**

▸ **Clicking the Display Type button will give you some information about your graphics card, like what kind of chip it is using and how much memory it has. You can also use this button if you need to change your graphics hardware or monitor.**

 7 Once you've made your changes and successfully tested them, click OK. Depending on the changes, you may be told that the system needs to be restarted for them to take effect.

2 Double-click the Display icon. This will bring up the Display Properties window, with the Background tab in front. Click Settings, the rightmost tab.

3 The Desktop Area slider bar is where you can increase (or decrease) your screen resolution. Depending on your computer's capabilities, there may be one or more levels you can select. The greater the resolution, the more space you get, but the elements of your desktop get correspondingly smaller.

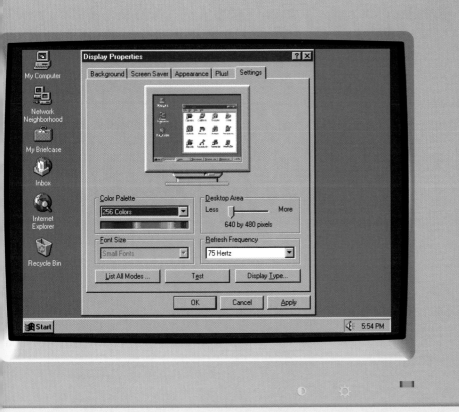

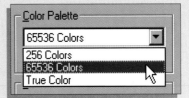

4 Choose the number of colors you want to display from the Color Palette menu. More colors look better, but may slow down your machine somewhat. If you select more colors than your machine can display at your chosen resolution, the Desktop Area slider bar will reduce resolution to the highest possible for those colors.

6 Click the Test button to test your choices. The Testing Mode dialog box opens. Click OK. This prevents you from inadvertently choosing settings that your machine doesn't support. If the test is successful, you'll see a color test image for five seconds.

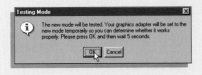

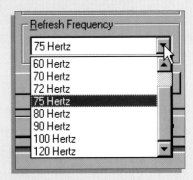

5 Select the refresh frequency you want. 75Hz is a good level because it is easy on the eyes and is supported by most computers.

How to Change the Screen Saver

In the old days, screen savers were used to prevent images that were displayed for long periods of time from being etched permanently into the screen. Nowadays, they're more for show than anything else, and screen savers are used primarily to give us (and passersby) something interesting and fun to look at while the computer is not in use. Windows NT offers a number of screen savers to choose from, and you can customize each to suit your own personal preferences.

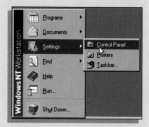

▶ **1** Click the Start button, place the cursor over Settings, and then click Control Panel.

[OK]

8 Once you've made your changes, click OK to confirm them and close the Display Properties window.

TIP SHEET

▶ **If you really want to impress your friends and coworkers, choose one of the first few screen savers on the list labeled OpenGL. These screen savers are displayed in 3D and are by far the best looking ones of the group.**

▶ **Be careful when password-protecting screen savers. You'll need to enter your NT user account password (the password you use when you log in) to get access to your machine.**

7 Click the Preview button. This will let you see the screen saver as it will appear when it starts on its own.

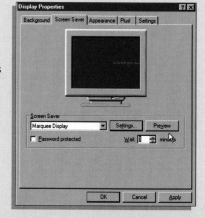

2 Double-click the Display icon. This will bring up the Display Properties window. Click the Screen Saver tab.

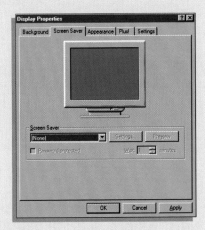

3 Choose the screen saver you want to use from the drop-menu list of choices. As you click each one, you'll be able to see what it looks like by looking at the mini-screen in the center of the window.

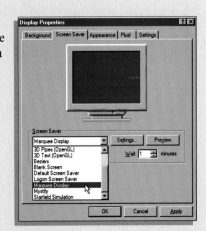

4 Click the Settings button to change the characteristics of the screen saver. In this example, you can type in the text that will appear across the screen. Click OK when you're done.

6 You can also use the screen saver to password-protect your computer. This will prevent strangers from using your PC when it's unattended. Click in the check box to turn on password protection.

5 From the Screen Saver tab, choose the length of

time you want the computer to wait before activating the screen saver. If you set the timer for 20 minutes, for example, the screen saver will activate after the computer has been idle for 20 minutes. It won't come on if you are working, however.

How to Set the Date and Time

K eeping accurate date and time information on a computer is very important. It not only lets you track when files were created or modified, but it also lets you know when it's time to go home. Your computer has a built-in clock so you often won't need to adjust this information. Sometimes, however, you will need to change it; for example, if you're working on a notebook and travel to a different time zone.

 1 Click the Start button, place the cursor over Settings, and then click Control Panel.

2 Double-click the Date/Time icon, which will open the Date/Time Properties window with the Date & Time tab in front.

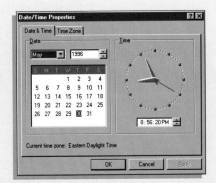

3 Verify that the date is correct. You can change the month and year by clicking the up and down arrows next to each. Then select the day by clicking it in the calendar box.

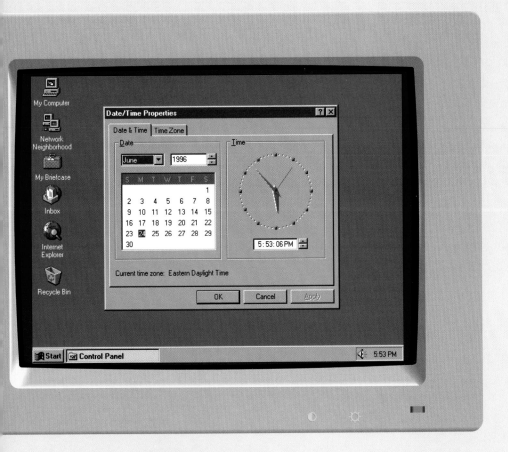

4 Next, check the time for accuracy. You can adjust the time by clicking the hour, minutes, or seconds value and typing in a new number, or you can use the up and down arrows to increase or decrease the value.

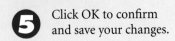

5 Click OK to confirm and save your changes.

How to Add and Remove Items on the Start Menu

The Start menu is a key part of the Windows NT desktop. It's convenient and easy to find, and as its name suggests, it is often the starting point for many operations, like launching an application, finding a file, or changing your computer's settings.

You can also put your own applications on the Start menu so that they are just as easy to reach. It's a good idea to put shortcuts to the applications you constantly work with on the Start menu, because you'll be able to get at them with a lot fewer mouse clicks than normal.

1 Click the Start button, place the cursor over Settings, and then click Taskbar. This will bring up the Taskbar Properties window.

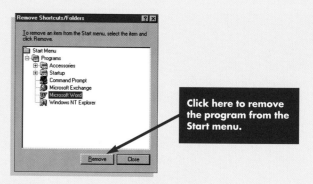

Click here to remove the program from the Start menu.

6 If you want to remove an item from the Start menu, click the Remove button. Click the program you want to remove, then click the Remove button again.

TIP SHEET

▶ If you click the Advanced button in the Start Menu Programs tab, you'll bring up an Explorer window view of the Start Menu. Here you'll be able to drag application icons from your hard drive to the Start Menu folder.

2 The Taskbar Options tab will be in front. Select the Start Menu Programs tab. To add a program to the Start menu, click the Add button.

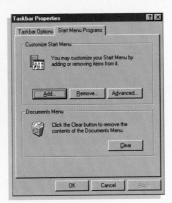

3 The Create Shortcut window appears. If you know the name and location of the program you want to add, you can type it into the space labeled "Command line." If not, you can browse for it by clicking the Browse button.

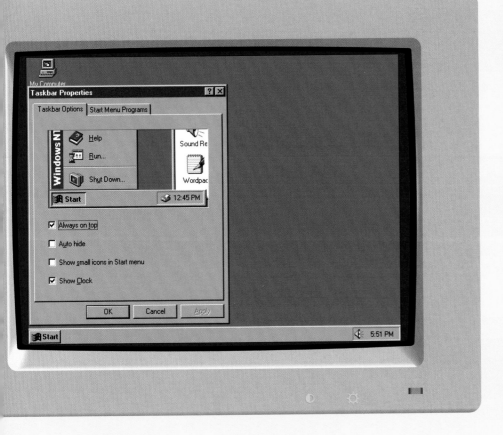

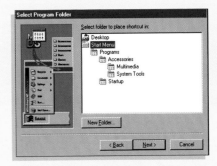

4 Once you've chosen the program you want to add, click Next. You'll see a list of folders where you can place the new shortcut. Click the Start Menu folder, then click Next again.

5 Now you can give the shortcut a name. Type the name into the space provided, and then click Finish.

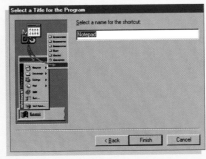

How to Change the Taskbar

The Taskbar is one of the most important parts of the desktop. It's the place in Windows NT where you can see which applications are running, and it is also the home of the Start menu. Because it is so important, there are a number of ways to customize it. You can change its size as well as its location. You can also change how and when it appears.

1 Click the Start button, place the cursor over Settings, and then click Taskbar. This will bring up the Taskbar Properties window. The Taskbar Options tab will be in front.

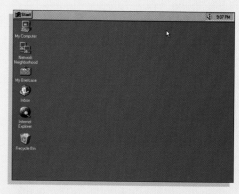

5 If you don't like the taskbar on the bottom of the screen, you can move it to the top, left, or right. Just click on a blank area of the Taskbar with the left mouse button, and drag it to your desired location.

2 Here you will see a number of options that control the Taskbar's behavior. For example, if you want to keep the Taskbar out of the way select Auto Hide. This will prevent the Taskbar from being visible unless the mouse cursor is moved to the bottom of the screen.

3 On the other hand, if you want the Taskbar always visible, click Always on Top. This will make the Taskbar visible at all times, even when application windows are running full screen.

4 You can also make the Taskbar taller. Just position the mouse at the top of the Taskbar so that the cursor turns into a two-headed arrow. Then click and hold the left mouse button, and drag the Taskbar to the size you want. You can make it as large as half of the desktop.

TRY IT!

In this exercise, you'll use all the customization tricks you learned in Chapter 11 to personalize your desktop. Specifically, you'll pick a background pattern for the desktop; choose wallpaper for it; apply a cool 3-D screen saver; pick a color and font for windows and dialog boxes; fine-tune icons and other elements; and tweak the Taskbar. Lastly, you'll learn how to change the display resolution and the color depth (the number of colors the monitor can display).

One last note: While doing this exercise, feel free to choose different settings than the ones you see here. They were chosen for the sake of example; pick the ones you like best.

Right click any blank space on the desktop. The context menu pops open; from it, choose the Properties item.

The Display Properties window opens with the Background tab in front. Here you can change the wallpaper and the desktop pattern.

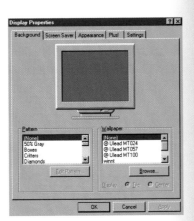

Let's choose a desktop pattern first. These are nice because they break up the solid monotony of the default desktop. Click different patterns until you find one you like; each is previewed in the Display Properties monitor. We chose Diamonds here.

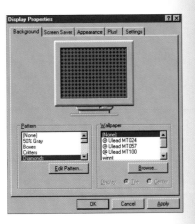

If you don't like a pattern as is, click the Edit Pattern button to modify it.

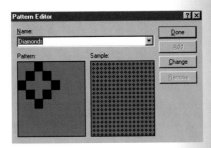

Each pattern is made up of two colors. When you click on a square, it changes color; the Sample window previews these changes. When you're done, click the Change button to save the revised pattern. Then click Done to close the Pattern Editor dialog box.

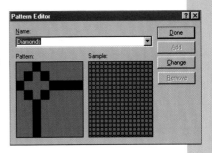

Wallpaper choices, like desktop patterns, are previewed in the Display Properties monitor. Select the one you like and decide whether you want the wallpaper image to be tiled (in which case it repeats until it covers the screen) or simply centered on the monitor.

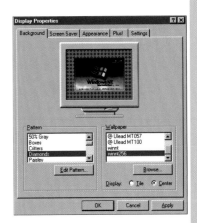

If none of the wallpaper suits you, browse for another bitmap image to use as wallpaper—you can use any bitmap on your system. When you find an image you like, double-click the file and the bitmap appears in the preview window.

Continue to next page ▶

TRY IT!

Continue below

10

You can also password-protect the screen saver to prevent other users from accessing your system while the screen saver is on. If you choose this option, you'll have to enter your logon password to access your system while the screen saver is on. In the Wait field, choose how many minutes of inactivity should elapse before the screen saver displays.

8

Now let's change the screen saver. Click on the Screen Saver tab, where you select a screen saver and see a preview. This example uses 3-D Flying Objects.

11

To see what the screen saver will look like, click the Preview button. We chose Two Ribbons.

9

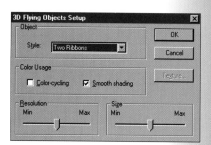

Click the Settings button to customize the screen saver. For example, you can choose the type of object that will be flying around on screen, and its resolution and size. Click OK when you're done.

12

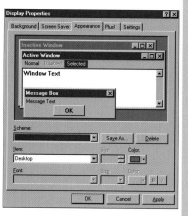

Let's move on to the Appearance tab, where you can customize the look of both windows and dialog boxes.

13

Windows NT comes with predefined "schemes" that combine different fonts and colors. Click on a scheme and it appears in the preview window.

14

Aside from selecting a scheme, you can customize individual components such as the Inactive and Active windows, the Message Box, even the scroll bar. To choose a component, click directly on it in the preview window; the component's name will then appear in the Item field. Choose the color and font you want to use for the item.

15

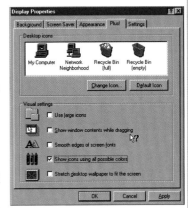

Next, click on the Plus! tab, where you can further enhance the desktop design with large icons and smoothed fonts, for example. Place a check mark beside the items you want. (For descriptions of the other options, click the question mark (?) in the upper right corner of the window; the cursor will turn into a question mark. Now click on any item under Visual Settings.)

16

Now click the Apply button to save all the changes you've made so far. They'll all take effect immediately and without closing the Display Properties window.

17

Next, click the Settings tab. Go to the Desktop Area. Use the cursor to slide the bar a notch to the right to increase the resolution. Here, we increased the resolution from 640 by 480 to 800 by 600.

Continue to next page ▶

TRY IT!

Continue below

 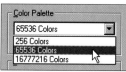

Go to the Color Palette area, where you can adjust the color depth. Click the arrow to open the pick list and choose the color depth you like—here, the color depth is being changed from 256 (8-bit) to 65,536 (16-bit) colors.

Click the Test button to see if you like the new color depth and resolution selections and to make sure they work—not all PCs support all resolutions and color depths.

After clicking the Test button, this dialog box appears. Click OK to begin the test. You might need to restart your computer for the changes to take effect; if you do, Windows NT will let you know.

The last task is to customize the Taskbar. To do this, right-click any blank area on it and choose Properties from the menu that appears.

When the Taskbar Properties window opens, the Taskbar Options tab is in front.

The Taskbar takes up room on your screen. If real estate is at a premium, you can click the Auto hide option to make the Taskbar invisible. To view it, you must move the mouse cursor to the bottom of the screen. When you do, the Taskbar pops up.

Click the OK button when you're done.

CHAPTER 12

Using Windows NT on Notebooks

 Although Windows NT 4 has the same look and feel as Windows 95, they differ significantly when it comes to mobile use. First off, Windows NT doesn't support power management: Simply put, that means Windows NT will drain your notebook's battery rather quickly, so don't expect to use it during a cross-country flight. Also bear in mind that to run Windows NT at a decent clip, you need a computer with hefty resources: *at least* a 486/66Mhz computer with 16MB of RAM. (The optimal NT 4 computer, however, is a Pentium Pro with 32MB of RAM. Windows NT 4 won't even run on a 386 computer.)

But perhaps the biggest drawback to using Windows NT on a notebook is its lack of support for Plug and Play PC Cards. Unlike Windows 95, which can automatically identify and configure PC Cards (and which lets you add or remove them at any time), Windows NT requires you to shut off your computer before inserting PC Cards. Why? Because Windows NT can only detect and configure them at startup.

In this chapter, you'll learn the ins and outs of setting up PC Cards; how to use Windows NT's Briefcase to synchronize different versions of files; and how to create hardware profiles.

One last note for those of you whose notebooks lack the horsepower to run Windows NT 4: If you're using Windows 95 on your notebook, you can still use the Briefcase to synchronize files with your Windows NT 4 desktop.

How to Use the Briefcase

One of the biggest problems with using multiple PCs is updating the many different versions of a file. Let's say you've got a desktop PC in the office and a notebook you use on the road. At the office, you begin working on a presentation, which you continue working on while travelling. This scenario inevitably produces two files: the older version in the office and the new one on your notebook. With earlier versions of Windows NT, you had to compare the time and date stamp of each file to figure out which was most up to date. Windows NT 4, however, includes a utility called My Briefcase, which automatically replaces the older version of a file with the new one.

▶ **1** Double-click the briefcase icon on the desktop to launch My Briefcase.

7 Drag the My Briefcase icon back to your desktop. Then right-click it and choose Update All from the menu that appears. The Update My Briefcase window opens and displays the files that need to be updated. Click the Update button and Windows NT replaces the old file on your desktop computer with the new one.

2 The first time you open My Briefcase, the Welcome to the Windows Briefcase window appears. Click Finish after you've read the information in the window and the My Briefcase window opens.

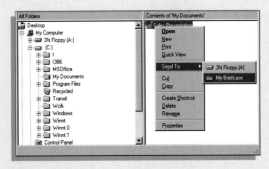

3 First, you must copy the files you want to work with to My Briefcase. This is a snap: From Windows NT Explorer, select the file (or files) you want to move to My Briefcase, then press the right mouse button. Choose the Send To option first, and then My Briefcase.

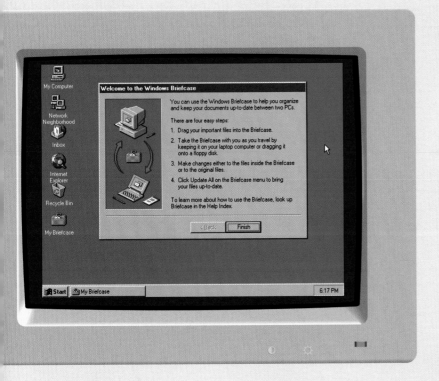

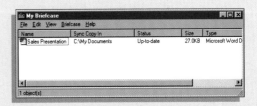

4 Double-click My Briefcase to verify that Windows NT has indeed copied the files there. Then close My Briefcase.

6 When you get back to the office, insert the floppy disk into your desktop computer's floppy drive.

From My Computer, double-click the A: drive; in the window that opens you'll see the My Briefcase icon.

5 Right-click My Briefcase, choose Send To from the menu, then select the floppy drive item. Windows NT then moves the Briefcase from the desktop to your floppy drive, so you can take the files with you on the road.

How to Use PC Cards

Almost every notebook computer has one or two PC Card (also known as PCMCIA) slots for inserting credit card–size devices such as modems, sound cards, and network adapters. Although Windows NT 4 looks a lot like Windows 95, it differs in several important ways that impact notebook users. First, Windows 95 supports a wide variety of PC Card models, but Windows NT 4's support is spotty at best. Second, Windows NT won't let you *hot swap* PC Cards, so you can't insert or remove them while Windows NT is running. Instead, you must shut down your computer, insert the PC cards, and then restart your computer.

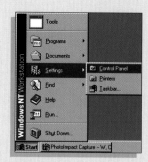

 Click the Start button. Then choose Programs, Settings, and Control Panel.

TIP SHEET

▸ Remember, you must shut off the computer before inserting or removing PC Cards. If you don't do this, Windows NT won't recognize the cards and they won't work.

▸ Windows NT comes with drivers for the most popular PC Cards. But some, particularly newer, PC Cards may not be on the CD-ROM. If that's the case, call the PC Card manufacturer to see if a driver is available; or, surf to the vendor's Web site, where you might be able to download the driver.

2 Double-click on the PC Card (PCMCIA) icon.

3 The PC Card (PCMCIA) Devices window opens and lists the cards that you've installed.

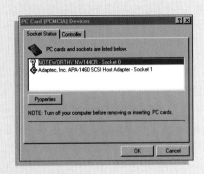

4 If the PC Card you installed requires a device driver, Windows NT displays a dialog box notifying you of this. For example, SCSI cards and network adapters typically require a driver, while modems generally do not. Click OK if your PC Card requires a driver.

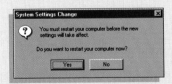

6 Windows NT now asks if you want to restart your computer. Click Yes. When your system restarts you'll be able to use your PC Card devices.

5 Next, you're prompted to insert the Windows NT CD-ROM. In the field labeled "Copy files from," type the directory with the files you need. On Intel-compatible computers (that is, on 486s and Pentiums), this is usually i386.

How to Use Hardware Profiles

Hardware profiles let you create and save different computer configurations. For example, let's say your notebook comes with a docking station, which you use when you're in the office. You can create a hardware profile that allows the notebook to use devices, such as a printer or network adapter, that are attached to the docking station. Simply choose that profile from a list of hardware profiles when you start Windows NT. To create a hardware profile, however, you must be logged on as the Administrator. And one cautionary note before you begin: Creating hardware profiles is easy, but figuring out how to enable and disable devices is really a job for techies.

▶ **1** Right-click My Computer and select Properties.

7 The next step is to change the device's status for a particular profile. You do this in the Device window by clicking the Enable or Disable buttons with the appropriate profile highlighted in the list of profiles. When you're done, click OK. Then click Close to shut the Devices window.

TIP SHEET

▶ **To change the priority of a hardware profile, select it, then click the up or down arrow on the Hardware Profiles tab in the System Properties dialog box. Profiles are listed in order of priority, with the highest priority profile at the top of the list. Clicking the up arrow bumps a profile up one level, raising its priority; clicking the down arrow moves the profile down one in the list, lowering its priority.**

2 In the System Properties window, select the Hardware Profiles tab. Under Available Hardware Profiles, you should see Original Configuration. Make sure it's highlighted, then click Copy.

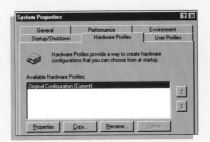

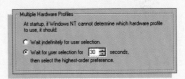

3 Now, you'll see the Copy Profile dialog box. In the blank space, type in a name for the profile, then click OK. When you do this, Windows NT makes a copy of the original configuration profile.

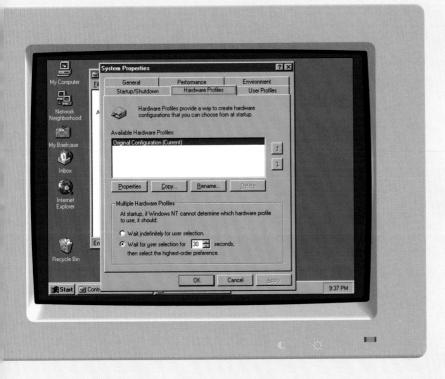

4 Now look in the Multiple Hardware Profiles section, where you have two options: You can either instruct Windows NT to wait indefinitely for you to select a hardware profile or to wait a preset length of time and then select the profile with the highest priority (see the Tip Sheet). Choose one of these options, then press OK.

6 Double-click the Devices icon to open the Devices window. At first glance, it may look intimidating: It contains a list of all the devices Windows NT supports, many of which have cryptic names. To change the status of a device for a particular profile—that is, to enable or disable it—just select the device, then click the HW Profiles button.

Devices

5 Next, open the Control Panel (by choosing Start, then Settings) and locate the Devices icon.

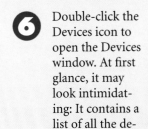

CHAPTER 13

Networking with NT 4

 If you're using Windows NT in the office, then your computer is probably connected to a local area network (LAN). A LAN is simply a group of connected computers that can share such resources as printers, files, folders, and storage devices.

In a Windows NT network, computers can be grouped into either *domains* or *workgroups*. In a domain, administration and security are centralized, which means all information is stored on one computer. In a workgroup, administration and security are distributed among all machines in the workgroup. For example, if you log on to a computer in a Windows NT domain, your account information (including the resources you're permitted to access) is stored on one central server. But if you log on to a computer in a workgroup, that information is stored locally.

This chapter shows you how to perform several key network tasks, such as accessing other machines on a network; adding a network drive to your desktop; locating another computer on the network; chatting and sharing folders with other users; and troubleshooting common network problems.

How to Access a Computer on the Network

Just as My Computer displays the drives connected to your PC, the Network Neighborhood displays all the other computers connected to your network. Using Network Neighborhood you can explore the content of these computers, such as files, folders, even printers.

▶ **1** Double-click the Network Neighborhood icon on the desktop.

TIP SHEET

▶ **To access a machine that's on the network but not part of your workgroup or domain, double-click the Entire Network icon.**

▶ **To identify whether an icon represents a workstation or a server, right-click it, and then choose Properties. In the General tab, look in the Type area. If the machine name includes the word "Primary" or "backup," it's a server. Individual computers, in turn, are simply called workstations.**

▶ **To access a network computer without launching the Network Neighborhood, just create a shortcut to it. First, use the right mouse button to drag the computer's icon to the desktop. Then choose Create Shortcut(s) Here from the menu that opens. A shortcut to the server now appears on the desktop.**

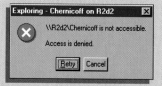

6 If you try to open a folder you're not authorized to use, a dialog box appears telling you that access is denied. Click Cancel to get rid of the window.

2 The Network Neighborhood window opens. It contains icons representing all the computers included in your workgroup or domain.

3 To examine the contents of a networked computer, right-click its icon and choose Explore from the menu that opens.

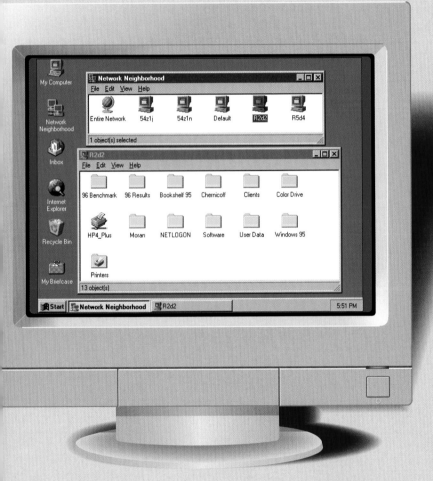

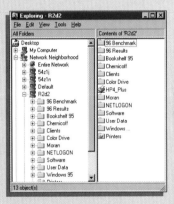

4 The Exploring window that opens displays icons for all computers on the network. However, the computer you selected is expanded one level: That is, all the shared resources it contains, such as folders and printers, are displayed.

5 To view the contents of a particular folder, double-click it. All the folder's contents then appear in the right pane.

How to Add a Network Drive

On the previous page, you learned how to access resources, such as files and folders, that reside on another computer on the network. If you frequently use this resource, you can save yourself a lot of time by *mapping* the drive to your computer.

When you map a network drive, NT assigns it a unique drive letter and can automatically connect to it when you log on; this saves you the trouble of repeatedly navigating the network to find a particular folder.

▶ **1** Double-click the Network Neighborhood icon on the Windows NT desktop.

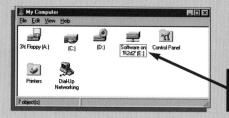

Mapped Network Drive

8 The last step is to double-click the My Computer icon. Inside, you'll notice that the icon representing the mapped drive looks different than the hard disk icon representing drive C. This indicates that the mapped drive is connected to the network.

2 Next, double-click the computer icon containing the folder you need. A window containing all resources on that computer pops open.

3 Right-click the folder you want to map, then choose Map Network Drive from the menu that appears.

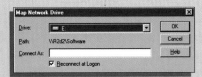

4 The Map Network Drive dialog box opens. Windows NT automatically selects the first available drive letter (in this case E:), though you can choose your own from the drop-down menu. (See the Tip Sheet for information on the Connect As field.)

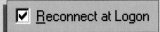

5 If you want Windows NT to connect to this drive each time you log on, click the box labeled Reconnect at Logon. One caveat: choosing this option can slow the logon process a bit. If you don't choose it, Windows NT connects to the drive the first time you access it.

7 A window pops up displaying the contents of the folder you just mapped.

6 After selecting the drive letter and deciding whether to use the Reconnect at Logon option, click OK.

How to Find Another Computer on the Network

If you're on a network with only a few computers, it should be relatively easy to locate a particular machine in Network Neighborhood. But if you're on a large network with dozens of domains and workgroups, you'll have to wade through them to find the computer you're looking for. The good news is that Windows NT has a Find Computer tool that can locate a computer anywhere on the network. The bad news is you must know the name of the computer you're searching for.

▶ **❶** Click the Start button, then choose Find. From the secondary menu, click the item called Computer.

▶ **Windows NT saves the names of the last few computers you searched for in a drop-down list in the Named field, so if you need to find the computer again you don't have to retype the name; just select it from the list.**

2 A window titled Find: Computer appears. In the Named field type in the *exact* name of the computer you're looking for (spelling of the name must be correct, but either upper- or lowercase characters may be used).

3 Click the Find Now button. Windows NT now starts searching for the computer you specified.

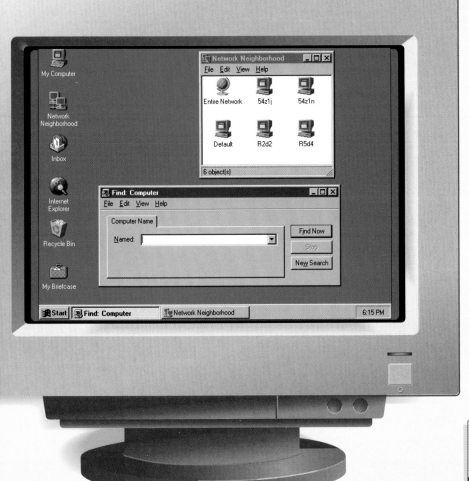

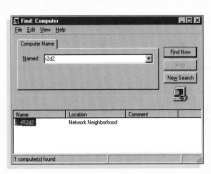

4 When Windows NT finds the computer, its name and location appear at the bottom of the Find: Computer dialog box.

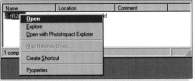

5 To open that computer, you can either double-click it or click the right mouse button and choose Open from the menu that appears.

How to Share a Folder with Other Network Users

There are a few prerequisites for sharing folders with other users: You must either be the Administrator of a domain or a member of a workgroup (where there's no centralized security). If one of these conditions is true, you can share any local drive: the hard disk drive, a floppy disk drive, or a CD-ROM drive.

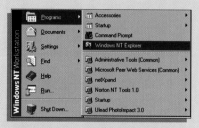

▶ **1** Click the Start button, then choose Programs and Windows NT Explorer.

TIP SHEET

▶ If you're sharing folders with DOS or Windows 3.11 users, limit the shared files' names to eight characters or less and don't include spaces. Although Windows NT 4 and Windows 95 support long file names, Windows 3.11 and DOS won't work with them. In fact, if you give a shared file a long name, Windows NT warns that some DOS workstations will be unable to access it.

▶ By default, Windows NT gives all users full control over shared folders, so they can read, write, and delete files from the folder. To globally change the rights for *all* users sharing a folder, from the Sharing tab click Permissions. This opens a window titled "Access Through Share Permissions." Now go to the Type of Access field, pull down the menu, and select the type of access you want other users to have: No Access (disables folder sharing); Read; Change (lets users change a file within a folder); and Full Control.

▶ To change the access rights for specific users (or groups of users), in the Access Through Share Permissions window click Add. Then proceed with caution: This is a complex task only experienced administrators should tackle.

2 Locate the folder you want to share, then right-click it. Choose Sharing from the menu that appears. (If the Sharing option doesn't appear, it means you're not permitted to share resources with other users.)

3 The folder's Properties window appears, with the Sharing tab in front. Now click the Shared As option, which activates fields where you can enter additional information.

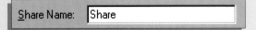

4 The Share Name field is where you specify the folder name as it will appear to other users. You can either leave the original folder name or type in a new one. However, entering a new name doesn't change the way the folder appears to you: When you view the folder within Windows Explorer, it's still got the original name (see Tip Sheet for more information about file names).

5 By default, Windows NT lets ten users access a shared folder at once. To limit the number of users to ten or less, click Allow in the User Limit area of the window and type in a new number, or use the arrows to change the number. Click OK. (Limiting the number of simultaneous users helps keep network traffic down.)

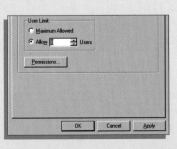

How to Chat with Other Users

Windows NT has a Chat utility for conversing with another user on the network: it works in real time, so as you type in your message, it appears on the other user's screen. And they don't have to be running Windows NT 4 either: You can chat with users running Windows 95 and Windows NT 3.51. Before you get started, however, call the person you want to chat with and ask the name of their computer, because the Chat utility requires this information. To uncover the name of *your* computer so someone can call you, right-click the Network Neighborhood icon, select Properties, and look in the Computer Name field.

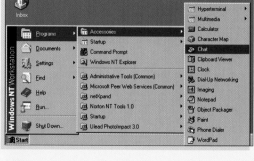

▶ **1** Click the Start button, then Programs, Accessories, and Chat.

- ▶ **To arrange the text windows so they're side by side, rather than stacked, choose Preferences from the Options menu. Then select the Side by Side option.**

- ▶ **To change the background color of your text window, choose Background Color from the Options menu. The Color window opens. Pick the color you like, then click OK.**

- ▶ **To change the font, from the Options menu choose Font. The standard Windows NT font dialog box opens.**

- ▶ **To chat with a Windows 95 user, you'll need to know their computer's name, too. If they don't know it, tell them to right-click Network Neighborhood, choose Properties, and then the Identification tab.**

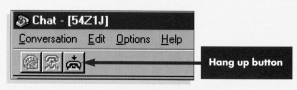

Hang up button

6 When you're done chatting, click the Hang up button on the toolbar. This terminates the connection.

Dial button

2 The Chat window opens. To initiate a chat, click the toolbar's Dial button.

3 In the Select Computer window, enter the name of the computer being used by the person you want to chat with. Or, choose it from the list of computers that Windows NT displays; on large networks, it can take a few seconds for this list to appear. After entering the name, click OK.

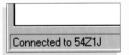

4 Windows NT then tries to connect to the other machine. If it succeeds, the message "Connected to [54Z1J]" appears on the status bar. If it doesn't, you'll get this message instead: "The other computer did not respond."

5 Once you're connected, start typing in the top portion of the window. When the other person types, their message will appear in the bottom half of your Chat window.

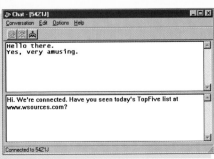

How to Troubleshoot Network Problems

Windows NT has a built-in help system you can use to solve common network quandaries. It asks you a series of questions about the type of problem you're having, then proposes possible causes. Although the help system won't solve every network ailment, it's a good starting point and definitely worth using before calling your network administrator.

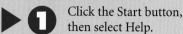

▶ **1** Click the Start button, then select Help.

TIP SHEET

▶ Some parts of the troubleshooter have shortcuts (indicated by embedded arrows) which launch the dialog box needed to fix the problem. Choose "I can't share a folder or printer on my computer," for instance, and the resulting window takes you to the Services dialog box.

2 From the Help Topics window's Contents tab, first double-click Troubleshooting, then the item labeled "If you have trouble using the network."

3 In the Windows NT Help window, the Network Troubleshooter appears. Under What's wrong?, choose the item that best describes the problem you're having. For example, you might be unable to connect to a specific computer.

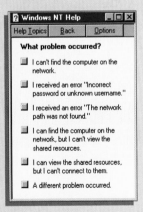

4 Windows NT then tries to troubleshoot the problem further. Choose the item that best describes the difficulty you're having, for example, "I can view the shared resources but I can't connect to them."

5 Windows NT suggests a solution. For the example above of being unable to connect to shared resources, Windows NT suggests that you contact your network administrator to ensure you're permitted to use that resource. Click Close Troubleshooter.

CHAPTER 14

Housekeeping and Gathering Information

 One of the strengths of Windows NT 4 is its ability to provide you with detailed information about all aspects of the operating system and the computer it's running on. It also allows you to manipulate applications and control the way they behave and perform. If you have administrator rights (which you probably do if you're running Windows NT 4 on a stand-alone machine), you can even create new user accounts and control what areas on the network each new user has access to.

In this chapter, you'll learn how to perform routine but important system tasks such as using the Windows NT 4 Task Manager, using the Windows NT 4 Diagnostics utility to tap into a treasure trove of useful information about your computer, adding a new user, and changing the performance of applications.

How to Use Task Manager

The Windows NT 4 Task Manager is a useful and powerful tool for monitoring what's running on your computer. With the Task Manager, you can see, at a glance, all currently active applications (also known as *tasks*), as well as a list of internal NT processes that are always running in the background as part of the operating system. The Task Manager also provides information about CPU and memory usage.

Although the average user will almost never need the more detailed information that the Windows NT 4 Task Manager provides, some of the information can be useful for diagnosing application problems. Task Manager also lets you close down applications that have stopped without disturbing anything else running on your computer.

TIP SHEET

▶ If you're a real techie and want in-depth information about each individual process running under Windows NT, click the Task Manager's Processes tab.

▶ You can increase (or decrease) the frequency at which the information in Task Manager's performance tab is updated. Select Update from the View menu, then choose from Low, Normal, or High (or Pause).

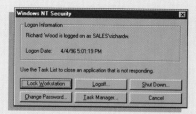

▶ **1** Simultaneously press Ctrl+Alt+Delete on the keyboard. This will bring up a window labeled Windows NT Security. Click the Task Manager button.

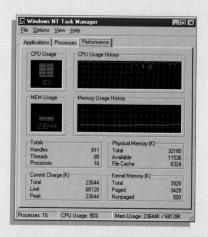

5 Click the Performance tab, and you'll be presented with in-depth graphical information about CPU and memory usage. Some of this information can be helpful when trying to diagnose system performance problems, though it may seem unintelligible to non-nerds.

2 On your screen you'll now see the Windows NT Task Manager window, with the Applications tab in front. It displays a complete list—like the one shown above—of all of the applications currently running on your computer. By double-clicking one of the applications on the list, you can bring its window to the front.

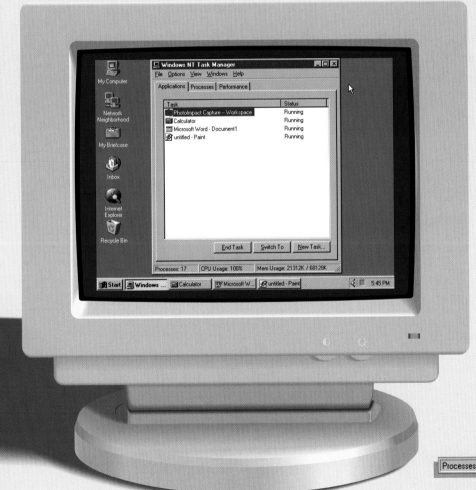

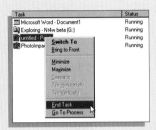

3 If for some reason an application has stopped responding to user input (such as a mouse click), you can end the task by right-clicking the application's name in the list and selecting End Task from the resulting menu. (You can also do this by clicking the End Task button at the bottom of the Task Manager window.)

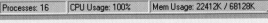

4 At the bottom of the Task Manager window, a status bar tells you how many processes are running, what percentage of your CPU bandwidth is in use, and how much of your system memory is being consumed. (The number of processes will almost always be higher than the number of applications you see in the list, because the former number includes parts of the operating system that run in the background.)

How to Get Information about Your System

From time to time, you may want to uncover information about your computer. For example, if you have a system problem and call a technical support hotline, you'll often be asked to provide information about your computer to assist with the diagnosis. Or, if you are technically inclined, you may just be curious about what's going on under the hood of your machine.

Fortunately, it's not necessary to take apart your machine to find out. Windows NT 4 comes with a built-in utility, Windows NT Diagnostics, which gathers information about your system, and presents it to you in a clear, easy-to-read format.

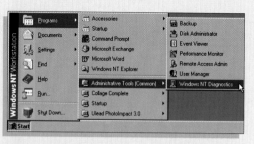

1 Click the Start button, then select Programs, Administrative Tools (Common), and then Windows NT Diagnostics.

TIP SHEET

▶ **Some of the tabs in the Windows NT Diagnostics window contain dynamic information that can change at any time. To make sure you're getting the most recent information, click the Refresh button at any time to update the data.**

▶ **If you want to save any of the information you discover in Windows NT Diagnostics for later reference, there are two ways to do so. First, you can save a copy of some or all of the information to disk by selecting Save Report from the File menu bar. Second, you can print a report by selecting Print Report. Individual tabs can be printed by clicking the Print button on each tab.**

▶ **If you're a power user, you may want to check out the three additional tabs, labeled Services, Resources, and Environment, which provide advanced users with even more esoteric technical information.**

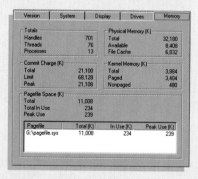

6 Click the Memory tab. This section provides a rather technical overview of the memory characteristics of your system. For most users, the point of interest will by in the Physical Memory section (upper-right corner), which displays the total amount of physical memory (the actual memory installed in your machine) as well as the amount available for you to run applications.

2 The Windows NT Diagnostics window will pop up. The first tab is labeled Version and tells you what version of Windows NT you are running as well as to whom it is registered.

3 Click the System tab. Here you'll see information about your system hardware, most notably your BIOS type and date (which is useful for troubleshooting some hardware problems), and the type of CPU you are using (in this case a 166-MHz Intel Pentium Processor).

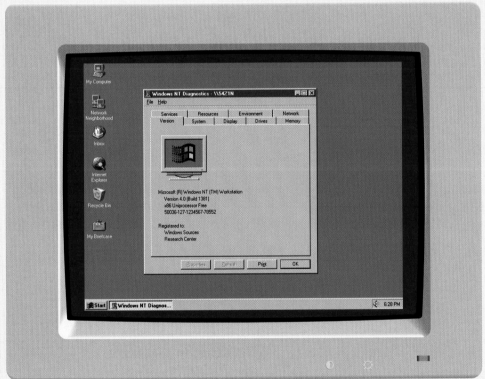

4 Click the Display tab. It contains information that is specific to your computer's graphics adapter. In addition to the BIOS date (which is not the same as the system BIOS), you'll find some detailed information about your graphics hardware, as well as driver information, such as the version number and the vendor name.

5 Click the Drives tab. This presents a hierarchical view of all of the drives in your system. You can click on the small plus sign to the left of the drive icons to expand each listing. Alternatively, you can click the Drives by Letter button to sort the list in descending order according to drive letter.

How to Add a New User

Windows NT assigns specific rights and privileges on the system to individual users. This means that several people can share a single machine running Windows NT 4, with each having customized access to system resources. For example, let's say user A (the administrator) creates a folder on a Windows NT computer that contains sensitive information. He or she can restrict access to that folder to certain users or groups of users so that unauthorized people won't be able to access that folder, even if they are logged on to the machine where the folder resides. (This security feature of Windows NT 4 requires you to run the NTFS file system.)

If you're using Windows NT 4 on a corporate network, you probably have a system administrator who controls who gets access to what. But if you install Windows NT 4 on a stand-alone computer, you automatically set up an Administrator account. This gives you the right to set up additional user accounts for people with whom you share your machine. Having separate accounts for each user enhances security, and allows each user to customize Windows NT to suit their own preferences.

TIP SHEET

▶ **For more control over the characteristics of a user account, select Account from the Policies menu on the User Manager's menu bar. An Account Policy window will appear, which lets you specify the password's length and age (how often it needs to be changed), among other things.**

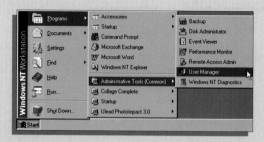

▶ **1** Click the Start button, then select Programs, Administrative Tools, and then User Manager.

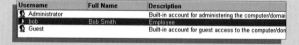

6 Click the OK button. You'll be returned to the main User Manager window and will see the account you just created in the user list. That account can now be used to let someone else log in to your Windows NT machine.

2 The Windows NT User Manager window will appear. The top half on the window contains a list of those using your NT machine. Every Windows NT 4 installation creates two users: Administrator and Guest, which is a built-in account for granting access to the computer without having to create a new user. (Guests have very limited access to Windows NT, though.)

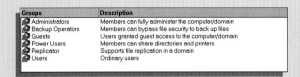

3 The bottom pane of the window contains a Groups list and a brief description of the rights of members of that group. Every Windows NT 4 user account must be a member of at least one group.

4 Select New User from the User menu. A New User window will appear, where you will enter information about the user account you are about to create.

5 Enter a username into the first blank field in the window. You can also enter a full name and description for the user. For security's sake, you can also assign the user a password by typing it into the Password field. You'll have to confirm the password by typing it again into the Confirm Password field.

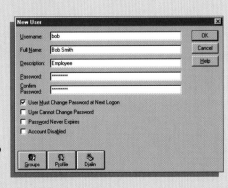

How to Create a Repair Disk

When you install Windows NT 4 for the first time, you are given the opportunity to create a *repair disk.* The repair disk contains backup copies of your Windows NT system files and configuration information. In the event of a system failure or a problem in which Windows NT refuses to start normally, the information on the disk can be used to correct the problem.

If you didn't create a repair disk at installation, you can still do so later (though the process is not documented very well). Here, you will learn how to create a repair disk for your Windows NT system. Before you begin, though, you'll need a blank, high-density, $3\frac{1}{2}$-inch floppy disk.

While the repair disk can often be helpful when you can't get Windows started, it is not a cure-all. It does not, for example, back up the contents of your hard disk (for information on how to protect your data, see Chapter 15).

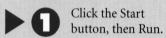

▶ **1** Click the Start button, then Run.

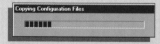

6 When the format is complete, the configuration files will be copied onto the floppy disk. Another status bar will appear. When the process is complete, close the Repair Disk Utility window by clicking Exit.

TIP SHEET

▶ Update your repair disk periodically, especially after some aspect of your computer's configuration has changed. To do so, click the Update Repair Info button in the Repair Desk Utility window.

2 Type **rdisk** into the blank space in the Run window, then press Enter (or click OK).

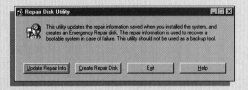

3 The Repair Disk Utility window will appear. Click the Create Repair Disk button.

4 A window will appear instructing you to insert a blank floppy disk into drive A. Do so, then click OK.

5 Windows NT will begin by formatting the floppy disk. A status bar will keep you informed of its progress. (The process may take several minutes.)

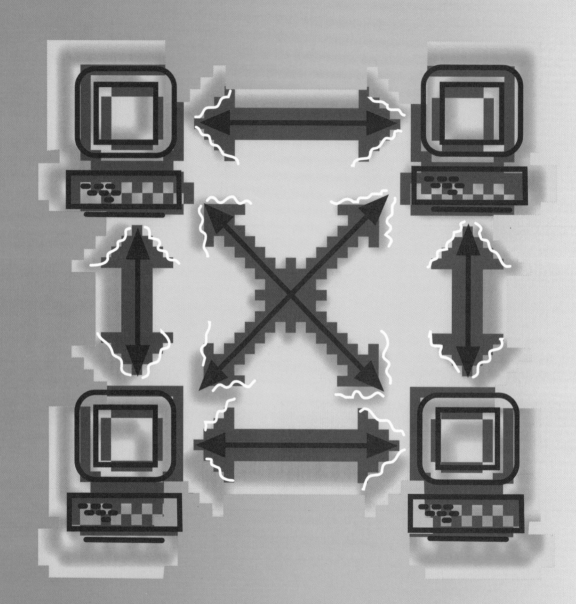

CHAPTER 15

Protecting Your Data

 Once you've installed Windows NT 4, customized it, installed dozens of applications, and created countless data files, you should seriously consider protecting your data. This will ensure that, in the event of a system failure or some other incident that damages or accidentally erases the contents of your hard disk, you can successfully recover your work with minimal time and effort. The alternative (doing nothing and hoping for the best) can be catastrophic, for it can mean the loss of days, weeks, or even months' worth of work with no hope of retrieving it.

An easy and inexpensive way to safeguard your data is to buy a tape drive and backup your data regularly. Backing up data copies information from your hard drive to a tape, where it can be safely stored until needed. This way, should something go awry, you can just copy the information back to your computer directly from the tape and save yourself a lot of worry.

In this chapter, you will learn how to install a tape drive, as well as how to back up and restore information from your Windows NT system. The day may never come when you need to rely on a backup, but if it ever does, you'll be glad you took the time to make one.

How to Add a Tape Drive

Computers are generally reliable, and most users tend not to think about problems until they actually occur. Although Windows NT is a very powerful and stable operating system, it is not immune to problems. Any number of factors can converge to make your system unusable. Common causes of system failure can include mechanical problems with the hard drive, unexpected and negative interaction between software products, or even a power failure. The key to recovering from such problems is to back up your data. The most popular way to back up data is by using a tape drive.

▶ **Windows NT 4 does not contain built-in driver support for every kind of tape drive. If your particular tape drive is not on the list, use the Have Disk button to install a vendor-provided driver. If your tape drive vendor doesn't include a Windows NT 4 driver, contact them by phone or look on their Web site for the driver you need.**

▶ **After you load the tape driver, Windows NT prompts you for a system restart so it can load the driver. Alternately, you can avoid restarting your computer by using the Devices icon in the Control Panel to manually start the tape driver. Find the tape driver in the device list (the name will resemble the type of tape drive you're using) and then click the Start button. Your tape drive is now ready to use.**

▶ **1** Click on the Start Menu, place the mouse cursor over Settings, and select Control Panel.

8 You'll be prompted that the machine needs to be restarted for the changes to take effect. Make sure you close down all open files and applications, and then click the Yes button. After your machine restarts, your tape drive should be ready to use.

7 Insert the Windows NT CD when prompted so that the appropriate driver can be loaded. Type the path to the driver (the \i386 folder if you're running on an Intel machine).

2 Locate the Tape Devices icon and double-click it.

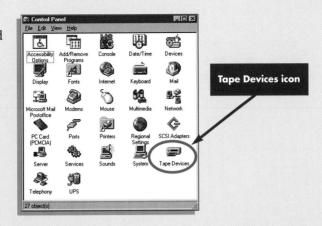

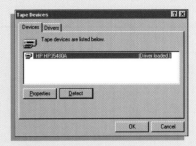

3 This brings up the Tape Devices window. Windows NT may already show your tape drive in the Devices list. If not, click the Detect button and Windows NT will try to detect your tape drive.

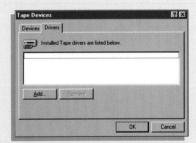

4 If Windows NT is unable to detect your tape drive, make sure that the appropriate power and data cables are properly connected and then try again. (You may need to restart the machine.) When it's detected the driver, click on the Drivers tab.

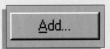

5 Click the Add button. Windows NT will compile a list of supported tape devices and present the Install Driver window, with drive manufacturers listed on the left, and particular models on the right.

6 Highlight the manufacturer and model of your tape drive, and then click the OK button.

How to Back Up Your Data

You may never have a catastrophic computer problem, but if you do, you'll wish you had backed up your data. If a hard drive fails, you could irretrievably lose everything you had on your hard drive—application software, letters, financial records, everything. Backing up your data is a good idea, because it can save you time and money when something goes wrong. Windows NT comes with built-in backup software that you can use.

▶ **1** Click the Start Menu, place the mouse cursor over Programs, select Administrative Tools from the resulting menu, and select Backup from the next menu.

6 Click the OK button to begin the backup process. Depending on how much information you're backing up, the process can take from several minutes to several hours. You may also need more than one tape.

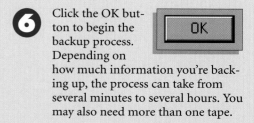

2 This runs the Windows NT 4 Backup application. The Drives window contains an icon for each hard disk on your system. Using the mouse, place a check mark in the empty box next to the disk you want to back up. This selects the entire disk for backup.

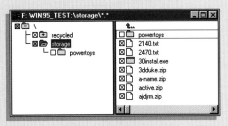

3 If you don't want to back up all of the data on the hard disk, double-click its icon. This will open an additional window which will display a tree view of all of the folders on that disk, where you will be able to individually select specific files and folders for inclusion in the backup process.

4 Once you've selected the data you want to back up, click the Backup button.

5 The Backup Information window is where you enter information and options about the backup. You can type a name into the Description window so that you can easily identify the backup later.

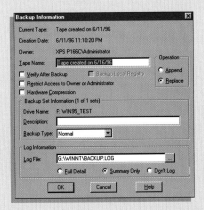

How to Restore Your Data

O nce you've made a backup copy of the information on your system, you should put it away in a safe place and hope you never need it. If the fateful day ever comes when you need to use your backup, you'll be glad it's there.

If you experience a complete system failure in which Windows NT won't work at all, the first thing you'll need to do is reinstall NT. After you've done that, you'll run the Windows NT Backup to restore the data to your machine. If you only need to restore a small amount of data (a small number of files or folders, for example) you can just go ahead and run the Backup program.

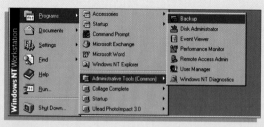

 1 Click the Start Menu, place the mouse cursor over Programs, select Administrative Tools from the resulting menu, and select Backup from the next menu.

▶ **You can have Windows NT write a detailed log file during the restore process. The log file will contain a comprehensive record of all of the restored files, as well as information about any problems that may have occurred during the restore process. By default, Windows NT only provides summary information in the log file. To have Windows NT create a detailed log file, select Full Detail from the Restore Information dialog box before beginning the restore. Here you can also specify where you want the log file to go.**

7 When the process is complete, you'll be presented with such information as how long the process took and how many files and folders were restored. Click the OK button to close the Restore Status window, and you're finished restoring your data.

2 This brings up the Windows NT Backup application. At the bottom of the window there is a small rectangle labeled Tapes. Double-click it, and it will expand into a two column window. On the left, you'll see the tape drive attached to your machine; on the right, you'll see any backups that are on the tape.

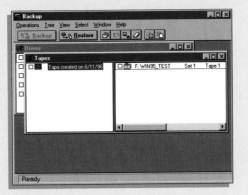

3 Click the check box next to the backup you want to restore from. If you don't want to restore the entire backup, double-click the small folder icon to see a list of files and folders contained within the backup. You'll be able to select them individually the same way you selected the backup.

4 Once you've selected the files and folders you want to restore, click the Restore button.

6 When you're done, click OK. This will begin the restoration process. The Restore Status window will pop up and keep you abreast of the status of the restore.

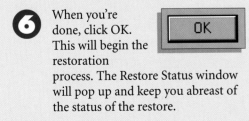

5 The Restore Information window will appear. Here you can specify the location where data will be restored, as well as customize various aspects of the restore process.

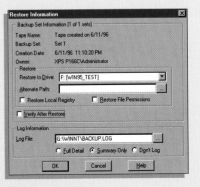

APPENDIX

Installing Windows NT 4 Workstation

 Some of you have been waiting to upgrade to Windows NT 4 from an earlier version of Windows. And some of you may be entirely new to graphical computing. Either way, Windows NT 4 was worth the wait because it boasts several major improvements over earlier generations of Windows.

The most notable improvement is Windows NT 4's new user interface, which is virtually identical to the one in Windows 95 and far easier to use than the user interface in Windows NT 3.51 and Windows 3.1. Changes under the hood are equally important. For example, NT 4 is faster and more reliable than Windows 3.1 because it's a 32-bit operating system. That means applications can use the physical memory (or RAM) installed in your computer more efficiently. The bottom line is that your applications will run faster. Windows NT 4 can also run multiple applications more reliably than Windows 3.1—a feature known as multitasking. As a result, Windows NT is much less likely to crash. And if one misbehaved software package does fail, it won't bring down all the other applications you've got running. Finally, unlike Windows 3.1, Windows NT 4 was designed from the ground up as a network operating system, which means it's easier to create a workgroup linking several PCs running NT 4.

What It Takes to Run Windows NT 4

All these powerful new features have a price, though: Windows NT 4 requires a faster processor and more RAM. For example, Windows NT 4 won't run at all on a computer based on a 386 processor. On a 486-based processor, it will run slowly. Getting the best performance from Windows NT 4 takes at least a Pentium processor (preferably a Pentium Pro) equipped with 32MB of memory. You also need a CD-ROM drive to install Windows NT 4.

If you're buying a brand new computer, Windows NT 4 will probably come pre-installed, in which case you don't have to concern yourself with the installation process. If you do have to install the operating system yourself, the process will vary depending on which version of Windows you're currently using.

Upgrading from Windows NT 3.51

The best way to upgrade from Windows NT 3.51 is to install Windows NT 4 in the same directory where NT 3.51 resides. Windows NT 4 will recognize your existing Program Groups, convert them to folders, and add them to its Start menu.

Upgrading from Windows 3.1

The best way to upgrade from Windows 3.1 is, again, to install Windows NT 4 over the earlier version of Windows, in this case Windows 3.1. Most of your Windows 3.1 applications should work fine under Windows NT 4. Windows NT 4 will recognize your existing Program Groups, convert them to folders, and add them to its Start menu.

Upgrading from Windows 95

You can't install Windows NT 4 directly into the directory where Windows 95 resides, as you can when upgrading from either Windows 3.1 or Windows NT 3.51. Instead, you must reformat your hard-disk drive and install Windows NT 4 onto a clean system. (Clearly, you must back up all your data before doing so.) Then you have to reinstall all your applications.

Choosing a File System

One of the first choices you'll have to make while installing Windows NT 4 is which file system to use on your hard disk. (The file system determines how information is arranged and accessed from your hard disk.) There are two choices: File Allocation Table, or FAT, and New Technology File System, or NTFS.

The best choice is NTFS, which has several advantages. First, it uses the space on your hard disk more efficiently and speeds disk access, particularly if multiple hard drives are installed in your PC. It also offers better security than FAT because it gives you more control over who can access files and folders.

FAT is the file system that's been around since the days of DOS and which Windows 3.1 and Windows 95 use.

Installation Options

Windows NT 4 offers four installation options (shown in the illustration below), and the one you choose depends on your needs and your computer's resources.

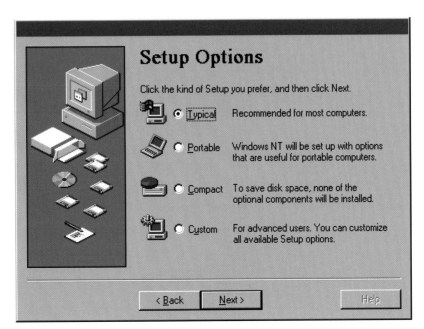

Typical. This install option is recommended for most computers. It installs the most popular and commonly used options.

Portable. This install option installs the features you need when using notebook computers, such as support for PC Card (PCMCIA) devices.

Compact. This install option is for those of you with limited disk space; it doesn't install any of Windows NT 4's optional components. You can install them later, though, using the Add/Remove Programs applet (see Chapter 3).

Custom. This option is for advanced users because it lets you pick and choose which components are installed. It also gives you precise control over all setup options.

INDEX

Y